Dear Sheila and Cyril,

Hopefully this will entice the both of you to visit us soon again, and this time spend some time with us. Have a safe trip home,

the Powells

3/15/91

FLORIDA
PORTRAIT

▲ *A family enjoys a picnic amidst the cypress splendor of Lake Magdalene, May 23, 1927. (Tampa-Hillsborough County Public Library)*

FLORIDA PORTRAIT

A PICTORIAL HISTORY OF FLORIDA

■

Jerrell Shofner

Photographs and captions compiled and edited by Milly St. Julien

Pineapple Press, Inc.
Sarasota, Florida

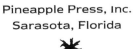

Published by Pineapple Press, Inc.

Inquiries should be addressed to Pineapple Press, Inc., P.O. Drawer
16008, Sarasota, FL 34239.

Library of Congress Cataloging-in-Publication Data

Shofner, Jerrell H., 1929–
    Florida portrait / by Jerrell Shofner. — 1st ed.
        p.   cm.
    Includes bibliographical references.
    ISBN 0-910923-80-9 : $29.95
    1. Florida — History.   2. Florida — Description and travel — Views.
I. Title.
F311.S56   1990
975.9 — dc20   90-7004
                                                                                CIP

First edition
10 9 8 7 6 5 4 3 2 1

This book was made possible in part by the support of the
Florida Historical Society.

Design by Joan Lange Kresek
Composition by Hillsboro Printing Co., Tampa, Florida
Printed and bound by Walsworth Press, Marceline, Missouri

CONTENTS

Acknowledgments

Florida Portrait marks a milestone in the activities of the Florida Historical Society. This publication is the first of what will become a series of volumes on the history of Florida. It is appropriate that this volume reflect the breadth and scope of our beloved state from its pre-European days to the present.

Jerrell Shofner, the author, and Milly St. Julien, the photographic editor, have combined to create a unique book. It is as much a work of art as it is history. Readers will agree that *Florida Portrait* fills a long-standing void in the popular history of Florida.

Special thanks should go to a number of people for seeing this project through. Dr. Gary Mormino, former Executive Director of the Florida Historical Society, nursed it along at its inception. Former President Paul George provided valuable leadership during his tenure of office.

The extraordinary efforts of the Florida Historical Society's Publications Committee produced the final product. Chairman Wright Langley, Dr. Marinus Latour, Stuart McIver, current President Hampton Dunn, and Milton Jones, the Society's attorney, provided close supervision and counsel. The Executive Director, Dr. Nick Wynne, also assisted the Committee. Ann Carroll and Carolyn J. Barnes worked diligently to index this work.

The sponsors of *Florida Portrait* deserve special thanks for their patience in seeing this project through to completion, for their ability to see the value of such a project, and for their willingness to commit dollars to see it through.

Hampton Dunn
President
Florida Historical Society

Prologue

A sandy protuberance jutting into the Caribbean from a land mass discovered five hundred years ago by Spanish explorers seeking another destination, Florida was at first more important for its geographic location than for its intrinsic value. One Spanish expedition after another found the region short on metallic wealth and long on native defenders. For nearly two centuries after Spanish discovery, Florida was regarded as an undesirable place, its sole value being its strategic location near the Bahama Channel, the Gulf Stream avenue connecting the Caribbean to the Atlantic over which the semiannual Spanish treasure fleets made their cumbersome way from the New World to enrich Spanish coffers in the sixteenth and seventeenth centuries. The peninsula's location meant that Spain must possess it so that no Old World enemy could. Florida thus assumed a significance in the international rivalries of early modern Europe disproportionate to the hardships of taming that hostile wilderness.

As Spanish hegemony declined in the eighteenth century and the treasure fleets became less important, Florida was held in such low esteem that Spain traded it to Britain for the return of the city of Havana in the 1763 Treaty of Paris and considered the exchange a favorable one. European rivalry for advantage in the New World declined markedly during the Napoleonic Age while an exuberant and expansive United States resolved to acquire Florida in order to quiet its southern border. Americans rushed into the northern Florida lands to grow cotton, but for many decades they eschewed the sandy peninsula. Some wealthy Northerners began taking advantage of peninsular Florida's balmy climate as railroad transportation became available in the late nineteenth century, but it was automobiles, World War II, DDT, and air conditioning in the twentieth century that transformed Florida into the attractive, populous, and rapidly growing state it is today.

Chapter 1

The Land and the
First Floridians

▲ *Timucuan Indians, inhabitants of northeast and central Florida between 1300 to 1500 A.D., drying their catch. For most tribes, meat was secondary to the consumption of maize and beans.* *However, coastal Indians such as the Timucuans depended a great deal on fish and other game indigenous to the area. (University of South Florida Library—Special Collection)*

◄ *Testifying to the artistic ability of the Key Marcos Indians, this figurehead of a deer is painted in blue, black, and white. The artist used tools made of barracuda jaws and shark teeth. (Historical Association of Southern Florida)*

*H*aving risen from the sea some 20 million or more years ago, Florida was shaped and reshaped by the sea over long periods as it rose and fell during the Ice Age. When the polar icecap grew, it lowered the sea level so that the peninsula was at times twice as large as it is now. When the ice melted, the sea rose and washed against the land at a higher level. There are eight identifiable terraces between the central highlands and the present shoreline where the water left its mark. The present contours of the state took shape during the last 30,000 years.

As the land mass was being formed, it was inhabited by numerous prehistoric animals including the now-extinct mastodons, saber-toothed tigers, and great sloths, as well as spectacled bears, horses, wolves, and alligators. Although little is known about these extinct species, paleontologists are continually adding to their story. Digging in a pit in Marion County in early 1987, they discovered a skeleton of a 7-million-year-old mastodon that is believed to be the world's largest such specimen. Similar discoveries have been made in deep springs around the state and in several of the rivers. Many of these animal species were still present for several thousand years after the first humans came to the peninsula.

The Arrival of Man

It is believed that man first crossed over from Asia to North America via a land bridge connecting Siberia to Alaska about 35,000 years ago and reached Florida within the last 12,000 years. These first arrivals, known as Paleo-Indians, were nomadic hunters and gatherers who used primitive but deadly spears to kill even the largest animals with relative ease. Some authorities believe that the Paleo-Indians may have been so successful in their hunts that they caused the extinction of some species. Camping near water holes or river crossings frequented by the animals, these early Floridians stalked and killed their prey for the necessities of life. The meat supplied food, the skins provided clothing, and the bones and sinews were used for tools. These people also gathered nuts, berries, and some wild plants for food. There was little change in their nomadic way of life for several thousand years.

Cultural Changes

Most of the large animals disappeared about 8,000 or 9,000 years ago and the lifestyle of the Indians changed accordingly. While they still hunted deer and gathered nuts and berries, these so-called Archaic Indians depended increasingly on snails, mollusks, and shellfish for their food. They gradually became less nomadic, living in villages on the lake shores and along the streams for much longer periods than in the past. At times, however, the Archaic Indians did move, apparently to allow depleted shellfish to replenish themselves or to find better hunting conditions. Even while maintaining a semipermanent village, they frequently established temporary campsites for special purposes such as gathering nuts in season, hunting, or obtaining flint for their spearpoints. Living in the same places for longer periods than their predecessors, they accumulated more waste materials and consequently left a better record for archaeologists. That record is still quite sketchy, but more is known about the Archaic Indians than about those who came before them.

A Technological Advance

About 4,000 years ago a major technological advance was achieved with the invention of pottery. Fired-clay pots, tempered with palmetto fibers or Spanish moss, became available for storing supplies. Food gathering remained the same; however, it became possible for villages to be occupied year-round. Pottery designs and use became more diverse during the 1,500-year era anthropologists call the Orange Period.

Early Agriculture

The Transitional Period, beginning about 2,500 years ago, was marked by profound changes in the culture of Florida's early inhabitants. Excavations of sites throughout the eastern United States suggest that extensive trade, reaching far beyond present-day state boundaries, took place as early as the Orange Period. New ideas and new tools were spread widely as they developed. One such change was the introduction of agriculture. The people continued to hunt and fish and gather nuts and berries, but they also realized the advantages of cultivated crops. Squash was probably the first crop grown, but maize was introduced shortly thereafter. It was many more years, however, before either food became a significant part of the diet of Florida's Indians.

▲ *A Timucuan village sketched by French artist Jacques Le Moyne. (Florida Historical Society)*

Societal Arrangements

The social organization of these early Floridians is believed to have been quite egalitarian. Village chiefs were probably selected because of their abilities as hunters. A chief's influence did not reach beyond the individual village, and cultural similarities among villages never extended to political unity.

During the Transitional Period, the people inhabiting the St. Johns River valley and the central Florida lake region were distinguishable enough from other cultural groups to be called the St. Johns people. They traded with other groups and continued to hunt and gather as well as grow squash and maize. With the introduction of an improved variety of maize, that food became much more important in their diet after about 800–1000 A.D. Probably influenced by ideas from other cultural groups with whom they traded, the St. Johns people developed an elaborate ritual for treating their dead. Burial mounds were built in which the dead were placed to rest along with many of the artifacts they had used in life. Among those artifacts were ceramics containing materials unavailable in Florida that had been obtained through trade from distant cultures. Such finds have enabled modern archaeologists to learn much more about these early people. The St. Johns culture lasted until Europeans first began exploring North America. The Timucuan tribes of northeast Florida are believed to have descended from this group.

The Deptford Culture

A people identified as the Deptford Culture, distinguished by their pottery which was stamped or checked by wooden paddles, inhabited the entire area of western Florida and extended as far south as Tampa Bay from about 500 B.C. These people also buried their dead in mounds with elaborate ceremony. With the bodies have been found copper beads from the Great Lakes area, stone ornaments from northern Georgia, and pots and ornaments obtained through trade with groups all over the eastern United States.

The Fort Walton People

Because of the extensive trade and the resulting free flow of ideas, the Deptford Culture evolved into several distinct subgroups. With the introduction of beans and an improved variety of maize around 800–1000 A.D., the Fort Walton Culture appeared, extending from about St. Vincent Island to the Tallahassee Hills and northward. Essentially a riverine culture, its villages have been found along the coast and up the Apalachicola and Chattahoochee rivers. Although marine life was important to the Fort Walton people, they practiced a much more intensive agriculture than did their predecessors. The improved agriculture was accompanied by a sharp increase in population, and formerly egalitarian political arrangements gave way to a more complex ranking of individuals according to their roles. Leadership became hereditary. The Fort Walton people had central ceremonial sites usually surrounded by smaller villages and individual farmsteads. Some of the sites that have been discovered seem to have been permanent, while others were apparently occupied only occasionally as hunting and gathering camps when game, nuts, and berries were in season. Exchanges of goods and

▲ Recreation played an important role in Indian culture. Hunting and fishing provided pleasure as well as sustenance to the villagers. Young men trained for races, and the warrior with the greatest endurance won a prize. The ball game depicted here consisted of throwing a ball at a square target placed on the top of a tree. Games such as this developed dexterity and accuracy. (University of South Florida Library—Special Collection)

▲ If a town was burned due to a sentinel's carelessness, the accused was brought before the chief and punished by being struck on the head by a sharp-edged club made of ebony or other hard woods. Often the blow was so severe that the skull was split open. This form of punishment was administered for other crimes as well. Drawing by Jacques Le Moyne, c. 1564, and engraved by the Flemish artist Theodore de Bry, c. 1587. (University of South Florida Library—Special Collection)

ideas with distant groups continued. The Fort Walton Culture was still extant when the Europeans arrived. Both the Chatot of western Florida and the Apalachees of the Tallahassee Hills were part of it.

Early Inhabitants of Peninsular Florida

Influences of the Fort Walton Culture extended down the peninsula to Tampa Bay where the Safety Harbor Culture was a derivation from it after about 1400 A.D. The Tocabago Indians, living in the villages of Mocozo, Ucita, and Pohoy around Tampa Bay where they were later encountered by the Spaniards, were distinguished by their high degree of craftsmanship. Buildings were decorated with carvings, and seashells and pearls were valued as ornaments. An abundance of game and fish was supplemented by crops of squash, maize, pumpkins, and cassava to provide a rich diet for a thriving community.

The original inhabitants of the southern peninsula were somewhat isolated from their northern counterparts. The ancestors of the Tequesta established their villages along the coast from present-day Broward County to Cape Sable and in the edge of the Everglades, living primarily on the shellfish and mollusks that were so abundant there. Another group lived on the barrier islands between Charlotte Harbor and Cape Sable. Their villages were usually on the Gulf and they also derived their sustenance from the sea. This group, like those to the north, were mound builders and expended enormous numbers of man-hours constructing them for use in civic and religious functions. Their descendants were the Calusa Indians. A third group lived near Lake Okeechobee and obtained some of their food from the water. Unlike the other two southern groups, however, this group also practiced agriculture. They were eventually subdued by the Calusa and merged with them.

The People Who Met the Europeans

From a handful of nomadic hunters who reached Florida some 12,000 years ago, the first Floridians had come a long way by the early sixteenth century. Perhaps as many as 100,000 of them inhabited the area encompassed by the present state of Florida. They had developed complex social, economic, and political institutions, enabling them to defend their territories and carry on wars against other tribes. Jacques Le Moyne, the Frenchman who left his artistic renderings of the people he saw during his visit to Florida in the 1560s, described the warriors as tall, athletic, and formidable in appearance. With their bodies stained with vegetable dyes and tattoos, their hair coiled tightly on top of their heads, and armed with clubs and bows and arrows, they demonstrated to both Spanish and French soldiers that there was substance behind the appearance.

The huge mounds left by the early Floridians suggest their abilities to organize labor and to sustain construction projects over long periods. The remnants of their lives that have been excavated from their burial sites by archaeologists emphasize the complexity of their religious beliefs and practices.

By adapting to changes in climate and weather and to the disappearance of their major food supply, the original nomads had survived and flourished in intricate and highly developed cultures. They had learned to respect the elements even if they did not understand them and to use the land and the resources it offered without destroying nature's abundance. But these Floridians were about to encounter a culture which, unfortunately for them, had evolved to a degree incompatible with their own. Bringing dreams of wealth and conquest, their Old World rivalries, and strange diseases, the European invaders wrought havoc on the Indian inhabitants of Florida, most of whom were gone by the eighteenth century. The Indians left the land largely as they had found it. That could not be said of their conquerors.

Chapter 2

European Discovery
and Exploration
1513–1565

► *Although it is uncertain whether Don Juan Ponce de León actually believed in the legend, he is remembered throughout history as the man who discovered Florida while searching for the mythical Fountain of Youth. He began his career of exploration in 1493 as a member of Christopher Columbus's second expedition. The mythical island of Bimini, believed to be rich in gold and lying north of Hispaniola (Haiti), enticed de León to Florida. Reaching the east coast in 1513, he sailed around the peninsula to the west coast where he encountered hostile Indians. De León hastily withdrew and returned to Puerto Rico. Nine years later, de León tried a second expedition, landing somewhere on the central west coast of the state. Again met by unfriendly Indians and this time wounded in the fray, he set sail for Cuba, where he died in 1521. (Florida State Archives)*

◄ *De Soto's invasion of Florida as envisioned by a Dutch artist in 1706. (Florida Historical Society)*

FLORIDA

IV CENTENARIO DE

3 PTAS

PONCE DE LEÓN

CORREOS

ESPAÑA

F.N.M.T.

*S*ailing for sheer adventure, to promote the Catholic faith, to extend the possessions of their monarchs, and to secure personal fortunes—God, glory, and gold—Spanish noblemen with military training and more than their share of courage and daring set out for the New World in the years following Christopher Columbus's accidental discovery of the new land mass. Usually appointed by the Spanish crown as *adelantado* (governor), each of these *conquistadores* was a military commander, political official, and religious promoter in the lands he conquered. In less than three decades after Columbus's famous voyage of 1492, these remarkable men had subdued Santo Domingo and Cuba, crossed the Isthmus of Panama to the Pacific Ocean, and begun extracting enormous wealth in gold and silver bullion from Peru and Mexico.

Discovery of Florida

One of these adventurous noblemen was Don Juan Ponce de León, who had accompanied Columbus on his second voyage in 1493 before turning his energies to Puerto Rico. As governor of that island from 1509 to 1512, he built a town and established his authority there before being succeeded by Don Diego Columbus, Christopher's son. De León became intrigued with stories of Bimini, a fabled island north of Cuba believed to be rich in mineral wealth and the site of the miraculous and mysterious Fountain of Youth. Historians disagree about whether

Ponce de León actually believed the story of the Fountain of Youth, but none doubt that, having secured a patent from the king, he provisioned three ships for an expedition and sailed from Puerto Rico in search of Bimini in early 1513.

Sighting land on April 2, de León landed somewhere along the coast near present-day St. Augustine and named the land *Pascua Florida*. Heading south along the coast a few days later, the Spaniards encountered a strong current flowing northward. This was the Gulf Stream, which flows out of the Gulf of Mexico through the Florida Keys and along the Atlantic Coast before turning out to sea near Jacksonville and carrying warm water all the way to the North Atlantic off Scandinavia. It was this stream, also known as the Bahama Channel, that ultimately carried the Spanish treasure fleets on their semiannual journeys from the New World and thus made Florida an integral part of Spain's far-reaching empire. De León's expedition continued southward, rounded the tip of the peninsula through the Keys, and made land on the west coast near Charlotte Harbor. After a three-week stay, the Spaniards withdrew hastily rather than do battle with a force of about eighty Indian warriors who approached their vessels in canoes.

No Place to Land

Nine years elapsed before Ponce de León was able to return to Florida, but in 1521 he set out in two vessels with two hundred soldiers, several missionary priests, and an assignment to establish a colony. Again landing near Charlotte Harbor, he was immediately met with a devastating attack by the natives, forcing his retreat. De León himself suffered a leg wound that became infected and cost him his life in July 1521. He thus became the first in a long line of valiant Spanish *conquistadores* who found Florida and its fierce inhabitants too much for him.

Narvaez's Search for Treasure

Having seen for himself the fabulous riches of Mexico while accompanying Hernando Cortés to that land in 1519, Pánfilo de Narvaez obtained from the Spanish crown a patent to explore and settle Florida. Sailing from Cuba with about four hundred men and four vessels, he endured two major hurricanes before putting ashore somewhere near Tampa Bay in April 1528. Within a few days he had entered the Tocabago village of Ucita and added immeasurably to the growing legacy of Spanish cruelty toward the Indians of the New World. While his soldiers sacked the village, Narvaez sliced off the nose of Chief Hirrihigua. When the chief's mother protested, Narvaez had her thrown to the dogs. It is little wonder that when the Spaniards asked where they might find treasure, the hapless natives motioned toward Apalachee country to the north.

After a ceremony in which he claimed possession of the country in the name of the king of Spain, Narvaez marched north with three hundred soldiers and several priests in search of the promised riches of Apalachee while his ships sailed up the coast in search of a good harbor where the expedition was to rejoin them. But the arrogant *conquistador* would never see his ships again. After two months of plundering Indian maize fields and villages, taking prisoners to be used as guides and bearers, the expedition arrived in Apalachee territory. Though favorably impressed by the pine-covered hills and lakes of the panhandle, Narvaez and his men were disappointed to find only a simple village of thatched huts and no evidence of the promised riches. Enraging the Apalachees by occupying their village and holding their women and children hostage, the Spaniards were driven off by warriors armed with bows and arrows.

Weakened by the constant attacks and food shortages, the soldiers reached the coast somewhere west of St. Marks. Despairing of ever seeing their ships again and anxious to abandon the deadly overland march, they decided to build make-shift boats and head west along the coast in the hope of reaching Mexico. Using native wood, palmetto fibers, and the skins and hair of their slaughtered horses, they fashioned five clumsy barges. Shirts and other cloth were made into sails. In that fashion, the haughty Narvaez and his desperate force set sail.

The Ordeal of Cabeza de Vaca

One disaster followed another. Narvaez's own vessel was blown out to sea and lost. The soldiers in a second barge mutinied. The survivors were constantly under attack by Indians when they landed to find food and water. Ninety-seven of them eventually landed on the coast of present-day Texas, but only Alvar Núñez Cabeza de Vaca and three companions survived the first winter there. Convincing the natives that he possessed healing powers, Cabeza de Vaca remained in Texas for some seven years before he and his three companions made their way to Mexico before returning to Spain. One of his companions was the celebrated Esta-vanico, whose exploits as *El Negro* subsequently became part of Mexican folklore. The only other survivor of the Narvaez expedition was young Juan Ortíz, who had been left behind in Florida when his commander marched northward.

De Soto's Expedition

While Cabeza de Vaca was still making his way back to Spain, another *conquis-tador* was already planning to conquer *La Florida*. Hernando de Soto, a distin-guished member of a prominent Spanish family, had already amassed a huge fortune and a prestigious reputation from his twenty years in the New World. Having played an important role in Francisco Pizarro's conquest of Peru, he had recently returned to Spain with a desire for greater accomplishments.

De Soto had no difficulty obtaining an audience with Emperor Charles V, from whom he requested a grant to govern and exploit the land which comprises pres-ent-day Colombia. Instead, he accepted the emperor's offer of an *asiento* (contract) empowering him to pacify and settle the land stretching from the Río de las Palmas (Río Grande) to Florida. By that time, it was known that Florida was not an island, and de Soto's grant included that still unexplored expanse of land to the north. He was to spread the Catholic faith and govern the territory in the name of the Spanish crown.

De Soto's appointment came in May 1537, at about the time Cabeza de Vaca returned to Spain. De Vaca's unembellished, matter-of-fact rendering of the details of his travails not only failed to dampen the enthusiasm for de Soto's forth-coming expedition but seems to have stimulated even greater interest in it. De Soto was literally overwhelmed by petitions to join his party. As a result his became the largest and best-equipped expedition yet to depart from Spain to the

New World. De Soto sailed from Spain in 1538 with seven ships carrying more than 700 men; 250 horses; vast stores of food, clothing and arms; and a herd of 700 hogs.

After a stay in Cuba, where he had been made governor as part of the *asiento*, de Soto sailed for Florida, reaching the west coast on May 25, 1539, the holy day of the Festival of *Espíritu Santo*. In honor of the occasion he named the beautiful inlet at which he landed *Bahía del Espíritu Santo*. This site was probably Tampa Bay, although some historians claim it was Charlotte Harbor. Unloading his men, animals, and supplies, de Soto sent his vessels back to Cuba and marched into the hinterland.

Finding the village of Ucita deserted by inhabitants who remembered their previous encounter with Narvaez, de Soto burned the village to the ground, erected fortifications, and officially claimed the land in the name of Spain. Approaching the village of Mocozo, a detachment of his main force encountered a band of about twenty Indians. The Spaniards were surprised to hear one of them shouting in Spanish. He turned out to be Juan Ortíz, who had been living with the Indians since he had been left behind by the Narvaez expedition twelve years earlier. Having learned several Indian languages during his captivity, Ortíz readily agreed to become an interpreter for de Soto.

After departing Mocozo, the de Soto expedition systematically repeated the methods practiced earlier by Narvaez. As the troops approached a new village, they captured the chief and held him hostage. When the Indians surrendered, the Spaniards kept the chief captive until they reached the next village, where the process was repeated. Although they frequently encountered fierce resistance, the Spaniards were too strong for the natives and eventually overpowered them. Many Indians were enslaved for use as laborers, servants, and guides. Some were branded and they were often collared and chained together. Mutilation was a frequent form of punishment.

In this manner, de Soto advanced up the peninsula, pausing to celebrate Christmas on the shores of present-day Lake Jackson in Apalachee territory. After about nine months in Florida, and still hearing that great treasures were to

▲ Alvar Núñez Cabeza de Vaca, high sheriff and chronicler of Panfilo de Narvaez's expedition to Florida, arrived on the Pinellas peninsula on April 16, 1528. Along with Narvaez and his men, Cabeza de Vaca marched inland, and after months of aimless wandering and senseless rampage, the expedition stopped near St. Marks. The ill-fated expedition ended in disaster as all but four crew members perished.

Cabeza de Vaca and three companions wandered for eight years before finding their way to Mexico. Upon returning to Spain, Cabeza de Vaca published his memoirs. Hoping to return to the New World, he petitioned Charles V for permission to explore the lands he had traversed, but the king had already granted that right to Hernando de Soto. (Florida State Archives)

▲ Hernando de Soto, a Spanish explorer, amassed great wealth from his adventures in Peru. Expecting to repeat his success in La Florida, he put together a great armada and sailed from Spain. Landing somewhere on the central west coast of Florida and hearing tales of northern inhabitants with helmets of gold, de Soto plundered and fought his way across the peninsula. He found no gold and alienated the natives he encountered in his trav-

els. Over a period of three years, his expedition explored much of the area that is now Florida, Alabama, Mississippi, Tennessee, Arkansas, Oklahoma, and Louisiana. Eventually contracting a fever, de Soto died in 1541. His body was submerged in the Mississippi River—the Río Grande de la Florida, as he called it. His companions were left to find their way back to Mexico in 1542. (Florida State Archives)

◄ Spanish doubloons found near Vero Beach. (Pace Library—University of West Florida)

be had to the north, the Spaniards moved on. During the next two years they roamed over the present states of Georgia, North Carolina, Tennessee, Alabama, Arkansas, and Mississippi, leaving a trail of bloodshed and cruelty and tribes of angry and embittered natives along the way.

It was the land that finally defeated de Soto. After foraging for nearly three years over hundreds of miles, he had found no treasure, his supplies were exhausted, and his men had suffered many casualties and much disillusionment. De Soto himself contracted a fever and died in May 1542. His successor was Luis de Moscoso, who had been with him since the Peru expedition. Moscoso tried briefly to continue the treasure hunt, but he soon abandoned the effort and struck out for Mexico, arriving at Tampico with 310 soldiers and a few slaves in September 1542. While Moscoso gave a favorable report of the countryside his forces had traversed, enthusiasm about finding gold and silver in *La Florida* diminished markedly after de Soto failed either to find riches or to establish a permanent settlement.

Not only had hostile Indian resistance contributed to the failure of three ardent *conquistadores* to establish a foothold in Florida while others were finding fabulous wealth elsewhere in the New World, but the brutality of their Indian policy—which was being duplicated by their more successful colleagues—had caused a strong reaction in some quarters.

The Black Legend and a Peaceful Expedition

One of the primary goals of the Spanish crown in the New World was to spread Christianity by converting the native populations. While the priests had been unsuccessful in their efforts, they protested that the cruelty exhibited by the soldiers only made matters worse. The leading critic of the treatment of the New World natives was Bartolomé de las Casas, creator of the "Black Legend," according to which Spanish abuse of the natives was not simply injurious but actually genocidal. Accompanied by Father Luis Cáncer de Barbastro, who had experience among the Indians of Central America, Las Casas returned to Spain in 1547 and petitioned King Charles for permission to establish a peaceful mission.

With the king's blessing, Father Cáncer, accompanied by three other priests, a lay brother, and an Indian convert named Magdaleno, left Mexico for Florida in 1549. Despite Cáncer's instructions to avoid a landing on the west coast where the land was "running with the blood of Indians," the ship's captain, either by accident or intent, put in at Tampa Bay where indignant natives still remembered Narváez and de Soto. At first the Indians appeared friendly, but four members of Cáncer's party who had remained ashore after the initial meeting disappeared. Father Cáncer soon learned that a priest and the lay brother had been killed, a sailor had been enslaved, and Magdaleno had gone over to the Indians. After a strategy session aboard ship during which his remaining colleagues urged him to find another place to land, Cáncer resolved to stay. He had a small boat take him ashore where he had first encountered the Indians, but as he walked through the mild surf with his hands outstretched in a peaceful gesture, he was clubbed to death by the people he had hoped to teach. The survivors of the Cáncer expedition returned to Mexico.

The Dagger Pointed at the Spanish Empire

Enthusiasm for additional expeditions to Florida for personal gain or in the name of the crown or the church declined in the mid-1500s even as the peninsula became more important to the Spanish empire. Perhaps there was no gold in *La Florida* and the Indians certainly demonstrated no interest in Christian education, but the peninsula remained a constant threat to the Spanish possessions that surrounded it. The bullion-laden vessels that sailed from the New World to Spain twice each year were dependent on the Gulf Stream's powerful current to propel them around the tip of Florida and northward for several hundred miles before they turned eastward toward Spain. Threading the Keys and hugging the Florida coast as it did, the channel was exceedingly dangerous to sailing ships. Frequent storms and uncharted reefs took their toll and survivors of the wrecks were often stranded on the Florida peninsula. Rescue stations were needed along the coast. Moreover, there was always the danger that Spain's European enemies might see the advantages of a Florida base from which to attack and plunder the treasure fleets. Florida, it seemed, was a strategic geographic entity that Spain did not necessarily want but could not afford anyone else to have.

Protecting the Bullion Fleets

It was largely strategic considerations that prompted Spain's royal decree of 1557 authorizing settlements at the Bay of Ochuse (Pensacola) and Santa Elena (Port Royal) and charging Luis de Velasco, viceroy of Mexico, with responsibility for carrying them out. The viceroy turned to Tristán de Luna y Arellano to head the new expedition. De Luna was a wealthy nobleman with long experience in the New World and seemed ideally suited for the assignment.

De Luna gathered a force of five hundred soldiers and one thousand civilians and, abundantly supplied and equipped, sailed in thirteen ships from Veracruz in June 1559. His plan was first to establish a settlement at Ochuse and then to send a detachment to occupy Santa Elena. His mission was already in trouble before it landed in Florida in August: a hurricane had struck and damaged several vessels at sea. Another storm struck at Ochuse in September, destroying some of the ships that had not yet been unloaded. One of the surviving vessels sailed immediately for Mexico to seek relief. Meanwhile, scouting parties unsuccessfully combed the countryside in search of Indians from whom supplies might be procured. With the colony approaching starvation, dissension broke out; subordinates complained of de Luna's leadership, and some refused to carry out his orders. Suffering an apparent nervous breakdown in early 1561, de Luna publicly confessed his failure and begged the forgiveness of his followers. He was succeeded by Angel de Villafañe, who attempted to secure the Ochuse site with a small force and lead a detachment to occupy Santa Elena. But on his way around Florida, Villafañe also encountered a severe storm, forcing him to abandon the entire undertaking and return to Mexico.

The French Threat

Hearing the unpleasant news of another failure in Florida, King Philip II decided that no further attempts would be made to settle the hostile land. He apparently felt that if Spain could not succeed there, then no other nation could. But while the Spanish monarch was reaching that conclusion, France was already planning a settlement on the North American coast.

French interest in Florida was threefold. First, fishermen from that nation had been moving southward from the Newfoundland waters for decades. Second, France knew of the wealth the Spanish had been extracting from the New World and was eager to challenge that nation in any way possible, including attacks on the treasure fleets. Finally, French Protestants, or Huguenots, were frequently subjected to persecution at home and a colony in the New World might be a good place for them. Under orders from Admiral Gaspard de Coligny (a Protestant who walked a narrow line with his Catholic sovereign), Jean Ribault, himself a Huguenot, reached the mouth of the St. Johns River with his three ships on April 30, 1562. He named the stream the River May, planted a marker in the name of France, and traded with the local Indians, whom he found to be quite friendly. Ribault proceeded northward and left a detachment of twenty-eight men at Santa Elena, promising to return soon with reinforcements and supplies from France. But by the time he arrived in his home country, religious war had broken out there, and Ribault soon found himself in an English prison. The colony he left behind collapsed.

As soon as peace was restored in France, the crown sent René de Laudonnière to succeed Ribault. The new leader established Fort Caroline on the River May (which would soon be renamed the St. Johns River by the Spaniards). After initial harmonious relations with Saturiwa, a Timucuan chief who held sway over some thirty villages, the French were soon embroiled in the intrigues of the chief, the Utina, and the Potano, managing to alienate them all. Denied food supplies from the natives, the French garrison was shortly reduced to abject want and the colonists decided to abandon the fort and return to France.

While preparing for the voyage in a vessel of doubtful seaworthiness, the Frenchmen were surprised by a visit from Sir John Hawkins, the "Elizabethan sea dog" who had gained fame and fortune while plundering Spanish settlements in the New World and selling slaves he brought from Africa in a ship named the *Jesus*. In exchange for guns and ammunition, Hawkins left them a vessel more suitable for an ocean voyage.

Before they could sail out of the St. Johns on a favorable tide, however, the French were pleased by the arrival of a relief mission headed by none other than Jean Ribault, who had been freed from incarceration in England. Ribault's mission was most welcome to Laudonnière and his men, but the Spaniards were not so pleased.

Pedro Menéndez de Avilés

With an excellent spy network in Europe, Philip II had full knowledge of what the French were doing in the New World. He was determined to intercept the Ribault mission if possible and oust the French from Fort Caroline. Choosing Pedro Menéndez de Avilés, a sailor who had distinguished himself repeatedly on the high seas and who was then serving as captain-general of the treasure fleets, Philip charged him not only with the task of ousting the French but also estab-

◄ *Reaching Florida in 1562, Jean Ribault arrived with three ships and 150 colonists. Sent by Admiral Gaspard de Coligny to establish a French Huguenot colony, he landed at the St. Johns River, which he named the River May. Upon his arrival he ordered a stone pillar to be placed on the riverbank with the arms of France, the date, and his name engraved on the stone. Choosing to move north, the colony of Charlesfort was established at Port Royal, South Carolina. Returning to France, Ribault was caught up in religious civil war, escaped to England, and was imprisoned in the Tower of London because he planned to leave England without proper authorization. After his release in 1565, Ribault returned to France, where he was placed in command of a large reinforcement to assist Laudonnière's Huguenot colony in Florida. Here he encountered Menéndez's troops and was beheaded in October 1565. Although Ribault lost his life, his timely arrival saved Laudonnière and a few other Huguenots from certain death. (Florida State Archives)*

NIHIL OMNI EX PAR-
TE BEATVM ·

▲ *René de Goulaine de Laudonnière, leader of the French Huguenots in Florida, came to the New World with the Ribault expedition in 1562. After establishing a colony in South Caro-* *lina, Laudonnière returned to Florida as governor of the French colony. With an expedition of 300 colonists, he founded Fort Caroline near Jacksonville in 1565. Discontentment* *and treachery undermined his leadership and led to Laudonnière's imprisonment in his own settlement. He was restored to power shortly before Menéndez attacked the* *colony. Saved by reinforcements brought by Ribault, Laudonnière escaped Menéndez's wrath and returned to France by way of England in 1566. (Florida State Archives)*

lishing a permanent colony in Florida, an undertaking the monarch had abandoned only three years earlier. Partially as a reward for his distinguished service to the crown, Menéndez was named *adelantado* of Florida with authority to settle the land for his personal profit as well as for his king and church.

French Blood in the Sand

Reaching the Florida coast in late June 1565 with five ships carrying eight hundred persons, Menéndez sailed northward and stopped at a site he named St. Augustine. In early September he encountered four French vessels near the St. Johns bar. Seeing his force approaching, the French cut their lines and outran him. Menéndez returned to St. Augustine and prepared for a French attack, which came a few days later. But this time the weather was on the side of the Spaniards. While awaiting a high tide that would allow them to enter the river at St. Augustine, the French ships were scattered by a severe storm and Menéndez seized the opportunity to attack Fort Caroline. Marching in water often above their waists, his men approached the fort and breached the walls before its defenders knew they were in the area. All inside the fort except sixty men and the women and children were killed. During the next few weeks, Menéndez found the survivors of the wrecked ships along the coast. His methodical execution of all but sixteen of them earned the Spanish leader a notoriety for which he is still remembered. The inland waterway where the executions took place was named Matanzas Inlet (place of slaughter).

Within two months of his arrival, Menéndez—with considerable assistance from the elements—had scored a stunning victory over a superior enemy force and secured Florida for Spain. He had officially established St. Augustine on September 8, 1565, and was now free to see if he could succeed where so many others had failed.

Chapter 3

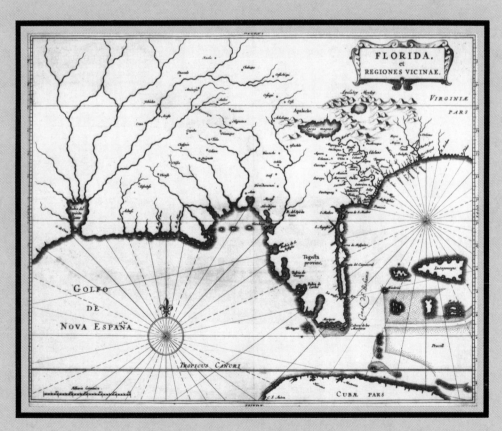

A Spanish Colony
and Anglo-Spanish Rivalry
1565–1784

Willow Oak.

◀ *A map of Florida drawn by the French cartographer Joannes de Laet in 1640. (University of South Florida Library— Special Collection)*

▲ *In 1754, the British naturalist Mark Catesby left a priceless account of the Floridas. This white-billed woodpecker on a willow oak is one of his illustrations. (University of South Florida Library—Special Collection)*

"Pedro Menéndez, of all his countrymen, not only conquered and explored Florida, but began in earnest to settle and organize it, and with a skill, an executive talent, which would have given Spain a much firmer hold on her colony during the following two centuries, had his successors been half as efficient as he was," according to the historian Jeanette Thurber Connor. Perhaps. Her assessment of his ability is certainly correct, but the task he faced was a mighty one. Menéndez had extensive responsibilities for protecting the Spanish trade routes in addition to his plans for settling Florida. He remained convinced that there was a water route through the newly discovered land mass and spent considerable time and energy searching for it. In the long run, after driving out the French, Menéndez succeeded in little more than establishing St. Augustine as a permanent foothold in Florida.

Spreading the Faith

Seeing one of his primary responsibilities as the spreading of the Catholic faith, Menéndez naturally turned to the church for assistance. Several members of the Society of Jesus came to Florida to establish missions, but they were unsuccessful. Father Juan Rogel, accompanied by a squad of soldiers, established a mission at Tocabago in early 1567, but by the end of the year, twenty-six of the soldiers had been massacred and Father Rogel abandoned his efforts. Father Francisco Villareal led a mission on Biscayne Bay for a short time, but hostile clashes

Castillo de San Marcos

Requiring more than 70 years to complete and costing millions of dollars, construction of the Castillo de San Marcos was surely the largest project undertaken in the New World in the seventeenth and eighteenth centuries. The oldest fort standing in the United States, the Castillo was built according to the design of Vaubon, the famous French engineer. It is quadrangular, with four-sided bastions at each corner and a moat surrounding the entire structure. Located to command the sea approach to St. Augustine as well as the only land access, which was from the north, the fort was equipped with a drawbridge and water and sewage facilities. With advance provisions of staple food supplies, it was a formidable structure.

Construction began in 1672 after the English had founded Charleston and a raid on St. Augustine had decimated about a fourth of the population. The fort was built mostly of coquina stone quarried from Anastasia Island and brought by a huge labor force to the construction site. Large numbers of Indians brought from as far away as Apalachee were employed along with numerous black slaves; many of the laborers were skilled artisans. Although the entire fort was not completed until 1756, the basic structure was in place by 1696— and that was fortunate. When Colonel James Moore destroyed the town in 1702, he was unable to penetrate the fort. James Oglethorpe also failed to capture it in 1739. In fact, the formidable edifice was never taken by an enemy.

The fort declined in importance after the British acquired Florida. Renamed Fort Marion by the Americans in the nineteenth century, it was sometimes used as a prison but for little else. In 1924 the site was made a national park and its original name was restored. Today, it is one of the major tourist attractions in historic St. Augustine.

---

between the Indians and the soldiers who were there to protect him soon ended that one as well. Menéndez made his greatest effort in Calusa country near Charlotte Harbor where he briefly enjoyed good relations with Chief Carlos. It was a tenuous harmony at best. When Carlos, in perfectly good taste according to his customs, offered Menéndez his sister in marriage, the Spaniard felt obliged to accept even though he had a wife in Spain. The unfortunate young woman never understood why her husband maintained a safe distance from her. The chief only barely tolerated the missionary even then. When Carlos became hostile, the soldiers killed him and named a new chief. When he too became recalcitrant, the Spaniards executed him and fourteen of his followers. With that, the Indians burned their village and vanished into the swamps.

By the time of Menéndez's death in 1574, the Jesuits had already abandoned Florida to work with the more amenable tribes of Mexico. They were succeeded by the Franciscan order, whose own missions in Guale (the region along the Atlantic Coast north of the St. Johns River) were decimated and five priests killed in a 1597 revolt. That disaster along with a destructive hurricane and flood in 1599 caused the Spanish government to consider abandoning St. Augustine altogether.

The Seventeenth-Century Missions

After a lengthy investigation, it was decided in 1600 that the site should be retained, but the resources which its proponents declared necessary to make it flourish were never provided. It remained little more than a military outpost for

◄ *A highly romanticized and inaccurate depiction of St. Augustine is shown in this wood engraving by Englishman John Ogilby, 1671. (Property of Robert W. and Alicia A. Harper, St. Augustine/St. Augustine Historical Society)*

▶ *An eighteenth-century map of Florida drawn by the Dutchman Pieter Vander. (Florida Historical Society)*

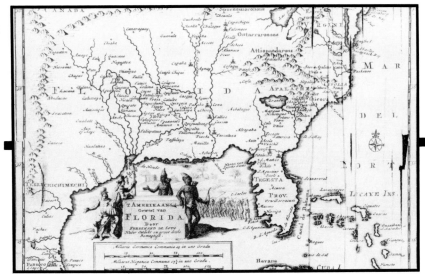

◄ *Arriving in Florida in 1743, the Jesuit priests Joseph María Monaco and Joseph Xavier de Alana reestablished a mission at the site of the abandoned Spanish settlement at Tequesta. The second village was named Pueblo de Santa María de Loreto. Despite a hostile reception from the natives, Alana and Monaco believed the mission would succeed. However, after only a few years, the priests were recalled by the Spanish monarch and the settlement was destroyed. This mural depicts a romanticized view of the Christianizing efforts; in reality, the Indians often ridiculed the Catholic priests and their religious teachings. Representing what might have been, the painting reflects Alana and Monaco's belief that with more soldiers to keep peace and farmers to till the soil, the settlement could become the largest in Florida. (Historical Association of Southern Florida)*

over 150 years. The mission system itself survived for a century as the result of a complicated arrangement between the Spanish crown and the Catholic church.

The king and the church had a close and mutually beneficial working relationship. According to the *patronato reál*, the king accepted the responsibility to finance and support the activities of the church, a duty from which the monarch gained obvious spiritual advantages as well as important temporal benefits. It gave the king the right to fill the church offices with his friends and he could determine the places where they would serve. But there were clearly established spiritual guidelines within which the monarch carried out this religious work. The nominal head of religious activities in Florida was the bishop of Cuba, but in practice he made only two visits—in 1606 and 1674—to the area in the seventeenth century. The Franciscans in Florida were led by a commissary general who was responsible for recruiting personnel for the missions and finding funds to pay their expenses. The bishop of Cuba, the commissary general, and the Florida governor often quarreled over the missions, and some of the governors were almost hostile to religious personnel. Religious authorities usually complained that the governors were parsimonious in supporting their activities. Governors were quick to claim that military personnel were required to protect the missions, and every religious person required financial support that could otherwise have been spent on a soldier. Moreover, the missionaries were constantly criticizing the governors and causing trouble while soldiers merely obeyed orders.

Although differing considerably in sizes of populations served, the missions were similar in physical layout and function. The church was the center of the site and governed the course of its daily life. Christian Indians attended religious services regularly, apparently impressed with the ritual. The priests taught the dogma and morality of the church and the converts worked the fields, some of which had already been cleared before the Spaniards arrived. Pagan Indians were a continuing problem, often taunting the converts and occasionally luring them away. Christian Indians frequently found the routine of mission life onerous and reverted to their pagan habits.

After the 1597 revolt in Guale, Indians there requested that the missionaries be sent back. By 1612 there were twenty-three friars serving twenty stations in Guale and Timucua. When the Apalachees asked for missions in 1607, Father Martín Prieto maintained contact with the natives of that region until resident missionaries were sent to the area in 1633. There were seven missions in that region when a violent uprising destroyed all of them in 1647. After Don Martín de Cuera's relief mission was defeated by the recalcitrants, friendly Apalachees themselves restored order. Twelve rebellious leaders were executed and others were condemned to labor on the fort at St. Augustine. This requirement was continued for the next fifty-nine years as a punishment for the revolt.

When Bishop Don Gabriel Díaz Vara Calderón came to Florida in 1674, he found eight missions in Guale, eleven in Timucua, and thirteen in Apalachee. There were 13,152 Christian Indians being served by some fifty Franciscans. The Apalachee missions became the centerpiece of the system. Although soldiers were permanently stationed at San Luis de Talimali near present-day Tallahassee and were frequently seen at the other missions, they were busy escorting traveling Spaniards as often as they were suppressing wayward Indians. The Apalachee

◄ *Sent by Menéndez to establish a mission at Tequesta (Miami) in 1567, Brother Francisco Villareal, a Jesuit priest, arrived in* La Florida *full of hope. At first, relations with the Tequestas were amiable and it appeared that the Indians welcomed Christianity; they even helped Villareal erect a large pine cross in the village. But soon the disgruntled Spanish soldiers accompanying the priest harassed and alienated the Tequestas. Villareal also discovered that conversion was no easy process— his only converts were among the very young or dying. Finally, the killing of a tribal elder by a soldier doomed the success of the first Spanish mission. The Spaniards were forced to flee to Havana a few months after their arrival. (Historical Association of Southern Florida)*

missions began trading with St. Augustine, providing the outpost with some of its foodstuff. While the missions were not an unqualified success, they had become permanent establishments providing an enduring and generally peaceful contact between the Spaniards and the native Floridians by the late seventeenth century. That stability, however, was short-lived.

British Threats to Florida

Although the territory's northern geographical limits were still undetermined, the Spaniards had long regarded Florida as comprising all of North America and all of Florida as belonging to Spain. By the late seventeenth century the English were expanding their claims southward from Virginia. Spain had slowly withdrawn her defenses along the St. Marys River on the Florida-Georgia border without recognizing the legitimacy of the English presence in the Carolinas. At the same time, the English settlers there were extending their trade into Apalachee country. When the Spanish attacked South Carolina, the English quickly retaliated. Then, when Spain and England went to war in the early 1700s, Governor James Moore of South Carolina seized the opportunity to attack St. Augustine in 1702. He burned the town but failed to capture the stone fort.

Facing severe criticism back home for his failure, Moore resolved to restore his standing with the South Carolinians by another attack on Spanish territory. With about fifty English soldiers and some one thousand Creek Indian warriors, he struck out for Apalachee. During late 1703 and early 1704, he destroyed a half-dozen missions, killed or captured hundreds of Indians, and left such a trail of pillage and torture that many of the surviving Indians began defecting to Moore and seeking his protection. After a brief respite, Moore returned to Apalachee in June and laid waste to most of the remaining missions. When he was finished, only San Luis de Talimali near Tallahassee and one other mission in present-day Jefferson County remained.

The End of the Missions

Moore claimed that he had either killed or captured five thousand Indians, although it is clear that some of his captives had gone willingly. In 1706 and 1708 the remaining Timucuan villages were raided, after which the only missions remaining in Florida were those near St. Augustine. In 1728 there were two villages reported in Apalachee, one with about 140 inhabitants and the other with only twenty. The survivors of that dwindling population were all that remained to welcome the Seminoles who began moving into the area from Georgia in the latter eighteenth century. The mission system was at an end, and the Spanish presence in Florida was once again reduced to the area around St. Augustine and its massive fort.

The French Again

While the English were pressing southward along the Atlantic Coast, the French were also threatening Spanish Florida. Fearing a French presence along the Gulf Coast, Spain decided to reoccupy Pensacola in 1698. Between 1699 and 1721, the outpost changed hands several times, but the Spaniards retained control of it, partly because the Bourbon family had acceded to the Spanish throne after 1715 and the two nations entered the famous "family compact," and partly because the French decided that their interests lay to the west in the Mississippi River valley. England continued to be the principal adversary of Spanish Florida for the next half-century.

The British Take Florida

From 1739, when England started the so-called War of Jenkins' Ear in the dubious defense of a pirate who displayed his severed ear before Parliament to demonstrate Spanish cruelty, until the Treaty of Paris in 1763, Anglo-Spanish difficulties in Europe were duplicated by their colonial rivalries in Florida and Georgia. After 250 years of exploration and attempted settlement, Spanish Florida in 1763 consisted of St. Augustine, a tenuous occupation of Pensacola, and a military contingent at St. Marks. When England and France went to war in 1756, Spain eventually sided with the latter. During the war the English navy captured and occupied Havana. In negotiating the 1763 treaty, France gave up her claims to North America while Spain willingly exchanged all of Florida—which then extended to the Mississippi River—for the return of Havana. For administration purposes, Britain divided the territory into East Florida and West Florida.

The Fish Legend

The exchange of flags required many months, during which general confusion reigned in Florida. Nearly all of the Spanish residents chose to leave, while British inhabitants were slow to arrive. There was a buyer's market for real estate and many of the Spaniards had to leave unsold property behind. Into the breach stepped Jesse Fish, an Englishman who had lived many years at St. Augustine as a representative of the William Walton trading firm of New York City. Offering to serve as agent for the unfortunate Spaniards, he acquired more than two hundred pieces of St. Augustine property, a 10,000-acre tract on Anastasia Island, and a partnership in a multimillion-acre tract near the St. Johns River. Remaining in Florida throughout the British era and into the second Spanish occupation, Fish became the largest real estate dealer in the territory and a major planter of citrus and other crops on the Anastasia plantation. Although oranges had been grown by the Spaniards, Fish owned the first commercial grove in Florida, shipping considerable quantities of fresh oranges and juice through the port of Charleston to Europe.

Despite his successes, Fish did not have an easy time of it. He was obliged to deal with the absentee landowners as well as the British and then the Spanish governments, each of which frequently questioned the proprietorship of his extensive holdings. The Spanish governor seized most of his St. Augustine properties in 1784, although Fish retained the Anastasia tract. He spent his last years as a recluse on the island, where he had moved to avoid the humiliation of an unfortunate marriage; his wife, Sara Warner, whom he had married in 1768 when he was in his late forties, had become "such a madcap" that he could not bear to witness her "imprudences." Fish died in 1790, leaving as many debts as assets, but the "Fish legend" lived on, gaining many embellishments over the years.

Governor Grant and the Indian Trade

The first governor of East Florida left a lasting mark in at least two ways. General James Grant, the second son of a noble Scottish family and an experienced Indian fighter from South Carolina, capitalized on earlier British successes and the corresponding Spanish failures in Indian policy. In cooperation with John Stuart, the agent in charge of relations with the southern Indians, he followed a policy of licensing private firms to trade, confining his official activities to holding conferences with them and exchanging gifts in demonstrations of friendship. Good relations were maintained partly because of Grant's wise policy and partly because of the Indians' desire for English trade goods. Under these circumstances, the firm of William Panton and John Forbes began trading with the Florida Indians—recently arrived immigrants who were retreating in the face of the advancing frontier to the north and replacing the aborigines whose ranks had been decimated. This policy was so successful that it kept the Indians loyal to Britain during the American Revolution, and the Spaniards were obliged to continue it when they returned to Florida in 1784.

▲ *The Spanish presidio on Santa Rosa Island in 1743. Spain regained the town of Pensacola from the French in 1722, but the Frenchmen burned the town before they departed. Spain rebuilt on Santa Rosa Island, and the Presidio Isla de Santa Rosa stood until a hurricane wreaked havoc on the settlement in 1752, forcing the Spaniards to return once more to the mainland. Engraving by Dominic Serres. (Pensacola Historical Society)*

PRISE DE PENSACOLA.

▲ *Under siege by combined Spanish-French military forces, Pensacola was a raging battlefield for over a month. British forces led by General Campbell were forced to surrender in May 1781. This engraving depicts the British defense of Fort George. (Pensacola Historical Society)*

Settling the Land with Englishmen

Grant also cooperated in the British policy of extending large land grants to persons who would try to colonize their holdings. A number of such grants were made, although some were more successful than others. Francis Philip Fatio established New Switzerland near the St. Johns River, and despite the difficulties of several changes of flags, some of his descendants still live in Jacksonville. Denys Rolle failed to make good at Rollestown further up the river, where he lost a small fortune.

One of the most magnificent failures, however, was the attempt of Dr. Andrew

The Battle of Pensacola

The Spanish never became an ally of the American colonies during the Revolutionary War, but they did agree to aid France, which was directly involved in the conflict. When Spain joined the French, it gave Bernardo de Galvez, the Spanish governor of Louisiana, an opportunity to conquer British West Florida. He first took Mobile in March 1780 and then launched his plans to take Pensacola.

After his first effort was thwarted by a destructive hurricane in October, Galvez again sailed for Pensacola on February 28, 1781. With some assistance from the French, he amassed a force of about 7,000 men and attacked the British post at Pensacola in early May. With some 2,500 white soldiers—some of whom were Loyalists from Pennsylvania and Virginia—and about 1,000 Indians, the British put up a stubborn defense, but a lucky shot exploded a powder magazine and caused such damage that the fort was surrendered in May 1781. Spain thus acquired West Florida by military conquest almost three years before both territories were ceded by the British in the 1783 Treaty of Paris.

Turnbull and several London investors to implant a Greek colony at New Smyrna. With about 1,500 Greeks, Italians, and Minorcans, Turnbull came to New Smyrna with high expectations and the blessing of the British government in 1768 to grow Mediterranean crops in Florida's balmy climate. During the first year, the colonists cleared a tract seven miles long on the Indian River to grow cotton, rice, indigo, sugar cane, and vegetables. Financing was inadequate, however, and some of the colonists became mutinous. The troubled colony was unable to resolve its difficulties, and Turnbull soon became embroiled in other problems that beset the colony as the American Revolution approached.

▼ Taken from Spain in 1763, Pensacola remained under British rule until 1781, when it once again returned to Spanish control. In the late 1760s, cartographer George Gauld drew this first perspective view of Pensacola. (Library of Congress)

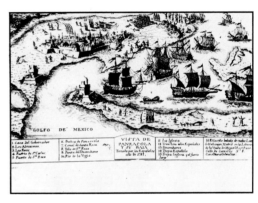

▲ Although geographically and otherwise inaccurate, this engraving was intended to provide a detailed portrayal of Pensacola Bay in 1781. (Pensacola Historical Society)

The American Revolution and Official Intrigue

Governor Grant left Lieutenant Governor John Moultrie in charge when he returned to Scotland in 1771 to assume the title left by his deceased older brother and the duties of administering Ballendock. Moultrie was eventually succeeded in 1774 by Patrick Tonyn, who was ill-equipped to deal with the explosive situation that bitter factionalism had produced in East Florida. Seeing treasonous intent in what was probably only political disagreement, Tonyn arrested Turnbull and freed the colonists from their indentures. The colony collapsed and many of its inhabitants moved to St. Augustine.

Meanwhile, the American Revolution was reaching a conclusion. Both the Floridas remained loyal to England while their northern neighbors fought for independence. While West Florida was beset by American raiding parties and attacks by Bernardo de Galvez, the Spanish governor of Louisiana, East Florida was more important as a haven for British Loyalists fleeing the revolutionary colonies than for military action. Between 1778 and 1783, East Florida's population grew from less than 5,000 to about 18,000 inhabitants. It was estimated that about 5,000 whites and more than 8,000 blacks had fled from the colonies to the north for the safety of St. Augustine. The population explosion caused major difficulties for Governor Tonyn's administration and sheer chaos during the lengthy period when flags were once again being exchanged.

Chapter 4

"Everyman's Land": Spanish Decline and the Emergence of the United States 1784–1821

► *Alexander McGillivray, known as Hopothle Mico among the Creek Indians, was born in 1759 to a Scottish father and French-Creek mother. True to Creek tradition, he received his education from his mother and her relatives. The Revolutionary War forced his father to flee to Scotland; Alexander remained among his Creek relatives. Recognized as a great Indian leader, he aligned his people with the British, remaining true to his father's heritage, and accompanied the Indians who helped defend Pensacola against Spain in 1781. By 1790, McGillivray believed the Creeks would best be served by a treaty with the United States. He traveled to New York City, where after months of negotiations, he and George Washington signed a treaty between the United States and the Creek nation. His death in 1793 deprived the Indians of a respected and talented leader, and in 1814, the Creeks lost the lands McGillivray had so ably protected. This portrait is claimed to be that of McGillivray drawn by John Trumball in 1790 at the signing of the treaty in New York City. (Pensacola Historical Society)*

◄ *An engraving of a Pensacola street scene in the 1790s, showing the importance of the shipping trade and the crude environment of one of Florida's larger cities. (Pace Library— University of West Florida)*

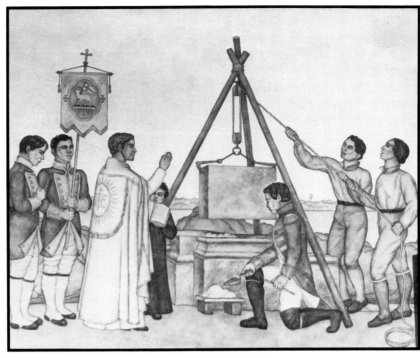

▲ Father Miguel O'Reilly dedicates the cornerstone of the Church of St. Augustine, c. 1790. When the diocese was established in 1870, the church became a cathedral. Its archival records date back to 1594. (Historical Association of Southern Florida)

*T*he Treaty of Paris of 1783 returned both East and West Florida to Spain, but the transfer was neither quick nor smooth. Suffering from declining power and influence since its zenith in the late sixteenth century, the Spanish empire was unable to reestablish control of its Florida colonies after 1784. Realizing that its exclusionary policies of earlier years had been unsuccessful, the government offered generous land grants to Americans who were all too eager to move to Florida—but who also had a propensity for bringing the U.S. flag with them. Unable to provide the trade goods that were essential to a successful Indian policy, Spain extended a monopoly to the Panton, Leslie Company, which for a time successfully carried out the delicate task of operating a British firm out of Spanish Florida and trading with Indians in both Spanish and U.S. territory. Throughout most of the thirty-six years of the so-called second Spanish period of Florida history, Spanish officials were barely able to administer the area immediately adjacent to St. Augustine. Filibusterers flying many flags and hundreds of Georgia planters occupied northern Florida with little regard for Spanish sovereignty. West Florida was in equal disarray during the period.

The British Exodus

The disorder during the many months required for the transfer of power also characterized the ensuing three and a half decades. Spanish Governor Vicente

Manuel de Zéspedes arrived in June 1784 to find departing Governor Patrick Tonyn vainly trying to maintain order in the countryside while directing the departure of thousands of Florida residents and Loyalist refugees. The change of flags was to occur in March 1785, but Tonyn did not leave until November of that year. The frequent differences arising between the two governors were slight compared to their common problems with lawless bands that were plundering the countryside.

Exemplary of the *banditti* was Daniel McGirt, a former South Carolina patriot who had allegedly defected to the Tories when his commanding officer attempted to confiscate his favorite horse. McGirt mounted his Gray Goose and fled to Florida, from which base he spent the war years raiding Georgia plantations, stealing slaves, and driving off cattle. When the war ended, McGirt—and others like him—continued to plunder, but they no longer distinguished between patriots and Loyalists. Tonyn had imprisoned McGirt at Fort San Marcos, but he had bribed his way out. When Zéspedes arrived, he offered a passport to leave the territory to anyone against whom British charges were pending. Some accepted, but McGirt preferred to remain and wreak havoc on the nearby plantations, including one belonging to Tonyn. Arrested and transported to New Providence, McGirt was back a few months later. The Spanish governor was not finally rid of him until 1795.

The Panton, Leslie Company

The decision to allow the Panton, Leslie Company to continue trading with the Indians was a fortunate one. By the early nineteenth century, the firm was operating almost as a banker for the hard-pressed Spanish government of Florida. But more important, the company was successful in keeping the Indians quiescent for years. The key to William Panton's success with the Indians was his friendship with Alexander McGillivray, a half-Scot, half-Creek, with whom he had become acquainted while both lived in Charleston. McGillivray had been educated in Charleston with the intention of managing his father's extensive business properties there, but both father and son left Charleston because of their loyalty to England when the revolution began. The father returned to Scotland and the younger McGillivray went west to become chief of the Creeks, a position he inherited through his mother's family. A natural leader and fluent in several languages, he was successful in organizing the Creeks, Chickasaws, Choctaws, Cherokees, and Seminoles into a loose confederation.

With the influential chief as a partner in the firm, the Panton, Leslie Company moved far beyond its original St. Augustine base. At the height of its success, the firm had stores in East Florida and at St. Marks, Pensacola, and Mobile. It also maintained outposts on the Apalachicola and Mississippi rivers. Such a successful enterprise was bound to attract competitors. After the revolution, American entrepreneurs out of the Carolinas began contending for the Indian trade, but the Panton, Leslie firm encountered its most serious threat from a Maryland Tory named William Augustus Bowles, who had come to Florida to fight for the British crown and stayed to join the Lower Creeks and to marry the daughter of Chief Perryman.

◄ Of Scottish and Indian descent, William Augustus Bowles came to Florida at the age of fifteen as an ensign in the British army. He lived with the Indians, learning their culture and sympathizing with their oppression. Bowles eventually married the daughter of Chief Perryman and became a supplier of munitions to the Creek Indians. Although a British subject, Bowles became the self-proclaimed director general of the Creek nation (Muskogee) and tried unsuccessfully to obtain British support in breaking the Spanish dominance of East and West Florida. He was twice imprisoned and died in 1805 while confined in Morro Castle in Havana. Original painting in the Bearsted Collection at Upton Park, Banbury, Oxfordshire; photo made from negative owned by Dr. J. Leitch Wright. (State Photographic Archives—Strozier Library, Florida State University)

◄ In 1792, William Bartram sketched the Indian Micco Chlucco and published the drawing in his Travels Thru East and West Florida. (Historical Association of Southern Florida)

▼ The Spanish governor's house on Intendencia Street in Pensacola, drawn by Pensacola resident Emma Chandler. (Pace Library—University of West Florida)

Director General of the State of Muscogee

Proclaiming himself "Director General of the State of Muscogee," Bowles terrorized the Panton, Leslie stores in West Florida between St. Marks and Pensacola before finally succumbing to Spanish treachery. With considerable ability and charm, the audacious and somewhat visionary soldier of fortune had ingratiated himself with many of the Lower Creeks and Seminoles—thus creating tension between himself and McGillivray and providing a base from which he and several British investors might take over some of the Indian trade. Many of the Indians were willing to trade with Bowles because they had become disenchanted with McGillivray's leadership and Panton's prices.

Having arranged for supplies from his British backers, Bowles set up shop in his newly announced State of Muscogee. One of his first acts was to march on Panton's store near the mouth of the Ochlockonee River, which he wanted to make his base. But the Spanish government, deeply obligated to Panton, forced Bowles to give up the trading post and invited him to New Orleans to negotiate a settlement. The trip turned out to be a ruse and Bowles ended up a Spanish prisoner in the Philippine Islands. His partners continued their intrigues in Florida, but no more was heard from Bowles until 1799. After a remarkable escape—he jumped from a Spanish ship off the African coast and swam ashore near Sierra Leone—the indomitable schemer outfitted another vessel and sailed for Muscogee. Although shipwrecked on St. George Island, he made his way to the mainland and regained the support of many of his former Indian friends.

With a price on his head offered by the Spanish, a suspicious observance maintained by the United States, and an ambivalent attitude on the part of the British, Bowles set about reopening trade between his dormant State of Muscogee and any firms willing to trade. He made his headquarters at Miccosukee, the most important of the Seminole towns, where the influential Chief Kinachee offered the greatest protection. Since Miccosukee was thirty miles from the coast, Bowles naturally needed a port. Without hesitation he marched on Panton's store at St. Marks, laid siege to the place for six weeks, and astounded the Spaniards by accepting the surrender of the fort there. A Spanish counterattack soon forced him out of St. Marks, but Bowles still seemed beyond reach as he retreated to the security of Chief Kinachee's Miccosukee village.

Bowles busily planned for the future. He established a navy to plunder Spanish vessels and used the booty to keep his Indian friends supplied. He welcomed runaway slaves from Georgia, and Miccosukee became a multiracial settlement. He wrote a national constitution, planned for a university, and tried to form an alliance with Britain. He also invited whites to Muscogee in the belief that his native allies would have to continue adapting to the white man's ways and that eventually their assimilation would be complete. Had Bowles had his way, Miccosukee would become the capital of a respectable nation, but that was not to be.

The Changing of the Guard in the Indian Trade

The diminutive Muscogee navy was gradually eliminated. Spain, the United States, and several Indian groups finally captured Bowles while he attended an

1803 meeting under a flag of truce. He was sent to Morro Castle near Havana, where he died in 1805.

In the meantime, William Panton died at sea in 1801 and his firm was reorganized as the John Forbes Company. The Indian trade continued, but the tribes gradually became hopelessly indebted to the firm. As a method of payment, the Indians ceded nearly two million acres of land between the St. Marks and Apalachicola rivers to Forbes and the Spanish government confirmed the transfer. The company gradually concentrated its trading interests at Pensacola, and the so-called Forbes Purchase became an unresolved problem for many years after the territory was acquired by the United States. Nonetheless, given its inability to supply the necessary trade goods for the Indian trade, the Spanish government's decision to permit the Panton, Leslie trading monopoly was a wise one.

The American Flag in Spanish Florida

The decision to permit Americans to take up land in Spanish Florida was not so wise. Governor Zéspedes had recommended opening Florida to foreigners, but he urged the exclusion of Americans. His successor in 1790 disagreed and Americans were included in the generous land policy. Thomas Jefferson apparently agreed with Zéspedes when he wrote "Governor Quesada, by order of his court, is inviting foreigners to go and settle in Florida. This is meant for our people. . . . It will be the means of delivering to us peaceably, what may otherwise cost us a war."

Between 1790 and 1804, the Spanish government granted hundreds of land parcels to Americans, who by the latter date composed the large majority of the population in the area between the St. Johns and St. Marys rivers. But difficulties arose almost immediately. When an invasion of Spanish Florida was inspired by Citizen Edmund Genet, a representative of revolutionary France, the Spanish governor blamed several American inhabitants of his colony with complicity, including John McIntosh, a former Revolutionary War hero who had established a successful business along the St. Johns River. Although no evidence of his guilt was ever brought to light, McIntosh was arrested, deported, and imprisoned in Morro Castle. His nearly blind wife launched a letter-writing campaign for his release that attracted the intervention of prominent members of George Washington's administration. The Spanish governor relented and McIntosh was released. Returning to Florida, the ungrateful McIntosh sent his family and property back to Georgia, and with a few accomplices, he destroyed the post at San Nicholas, burned Cow Ford, sank the Spanish ships anchored in the St. Johns, and then left the sands of Florida behind him, although he returned in 1812 to lead a revolution against Spanish authority.

The Spaniards finally ended their land policy in 1804 but not before another McIntosh had arrived. In 1803, John Houston McIntosh, a cousin of the impetuous man who burned Cow Ford, purchased the large Florida holdings of John McQueen and swore allegiance to the Spanish crown, although he lived most of the time in Georgia, where he had several other plantations. He too would eventually try to extend the boundaries of the United States southward.

The Enterprising Zephaniah Kingsley

Of the hundreds of Americans who moved into Florida during the 1790s and early 1800s, few were more successful and none were more colorful than Zephaniah Kingsley, who arrived in 1803 and lived at various times in St. Augustine, on his Laurel Grove plantation on the St. Johns, and on Fort George Island. One of Kingsley's sidelines was importing African slaves to the United States. He married one of his imports, allegedly a member of a ruling African family, and set her up in Florida in appropriate style as his wife. He not only recognized his children from this marriage but also others whose mothers were not so fortunate. Kingsley also became disenchanted with Spanish rule and joined the abortive 1812 revolution.

Acquisition of West Florida

The unstable border situation between Spanish Florida and Georgia, which had made Bowles's remarkable escapades possible, continued as Spanish power declined. After the 1803 Louisiana Purchase, American officials decided that the portion of Florida west of the Perdido River was really a part of Louisiana. President James Madison accordingly annexed it to the United States in 1810. Then embroiled in the Napoleonic Wars in Europe, Spain offered no resistance to the bold move. Encouraged by the ease with which the annexation had been accomplished, Madison and his advisers were spurred to additional action by a letter from Vicente Folch, Spanish governor at Pensacola, saying that he was willing to turn that territory over to the United States if he had heard nothing from his government by January 1, 1811. Madison was authorized by Congress in a secret session to occupy the Floridas if it were voluntarily delivered by local authorities—or to use force if necessary to prevent the territory from falling into the hands of another foreign power.

An Inspired Revolution

The United States was on the verge of war with England and was concerned about the potential threat of a large British naval force at Fernandina. Moreover, American officials were aware of extensive smuggling from that port into the United States and of the general absence of Spanish influence there. They were also well aware of the numerous Americans, such as McIntosh and Kingsley, who were living in the region and who were apparently anxious to revolt, declare the land between the St. Johns and St. Marys rivers independent, and ask for annexation to the United States.

General George Mathews, a former governor of Georgia with a distinguished military record stemming from the American Revolution, was assigned the task of accepting the Pensacola area from Governor Folch. When he arrived in Pensacola, however, the governor had changed his mind. Mathews then moved to East Florida and stationed himself on the St. Marys River while making plans to occupy northeast Florida under the guise of a local revolution. Once he convinced John Houston McIntosh and some of his allies that he possessed the blessing of the United States in his undertaking, Mathews received their willing compliance.

Given his standing as a major landowner, McIntosh was ideally suited to become the civilian head of the revolution. Within a few months his more martial cousin agreed to leave his Georgia home and lead the military phase of the movement. The formation of the Patriots of East Florida, conceived by Mathews and McIntosh, was intended only as a temporary arrangement. They planned to detach the northeast Florida area from the rest of the Spanish colony and declare it independent. Mathews would then accept governorship of the region in the name of the United States. In March 1812, members of the Patriot army crossed the St. Marys River into East Florida, capturing the territory between the St. Johns and the St. Marys except for Amelia Island. With the reluctant support of a naval squadron commanded by Commodore Hugh Campbell, who was uncertain whether Mathews had the approval of President Madison, the Patriots forced Don Justo López to surrender Fernandina on March 15. After accepting the surrender, McIntosh immediately turned Fernandina over to Mathews, who accepted it as American territory. The Patriots then marched on St. Augustine, but acting governor Juan de Estrada refused even to talk with them.

President Madison Repudiates George Mathews

About that time Congress denied further support to the president for the Florida campaign and Madison repudiated Mathews's entire operation. The old soldier was completely confused. After wandering around for several weeks, he decided to go to Washington, confident that a conference with his old friend President Madison would straighten matters out. But Mathews died of a heart attack at Augusta, Georgia, on his way north. In July 1812, the Patriots held a constitutional convention and named McIntosh "Director of the Territory of East Florida," but President Madison ignored them. By that time, the United States had been at war with England for nearly a month under an act of Congress passed on June 18, 1812.

Colonel Nicholls, the Seminoles, and Andrew Jackson

When Napoleon was defeated in Europe in 1814, the English were free to concentrate on the war with the United States. General Edward Pakenham and ten thousand regular soldiers were dispatched to attack the United States at New Orleans. Meanwhile, Colonel Edward Nicholls began supplying the Indians of West Florida and urging them to war against the United States. Several hundred runaway slaves and a number of free blacks were then living among the Indians, sometimes as nominal slaves and sometimes in separate villages. They shared with the Indians an antipathy for the American settlers. To Colonel Nicholls they seemed an ideal guerrilla force. Spanish Governor Sebastian Kindelán was afraid that Nicholls's activities would cause him difficulty with the United States, but he was powerless to stop them.

When the Creeks went to war against the settlers, many of the frontiersmen took refuge in Fort Mims near the Alabama River. The Creeks attacked the fort, killing most of the people inside. General Andrew Jackson marched his Tennessee militia in pursuit of the Indians, cornered them at Horseshoe Bend in 1813, and destroyed the fighting capacity of the Red Stick Creeks. The survivors migrated to Florida, where they joined the Miccosukees and other bands to become the Seminoles.

In a series of swift moves, Jackson occupied Mobile before the British could get there, captured and later evacuated Spanish Pensacola, and still reached New Orleans in time to defeat General Edward Pakenham's army at the Battle of New Orleans on January 8, 1815.

The Hero of New Orleans and the End of the War of 1812

With his Tennessee militia and a motley assemblage of volunteers including several pirates, Andrew Jackson prepared to defend New Orleans against Sir Edward Pakenham and ten thousand regular British soldiers fresh from the battlefields of Europe where they had assisted in the defeat of Napoleon.

As the redcoats marched upright into battle, Jackson's men crouched behind cotton bales and other defensive bulwarks and decimated the British ranks. The invaders retreated, leaving a large number of casualties, while Jackson lost only a handful of men. News of the sensational victory soon cheered the American people, who had had little cause for celebration during the thirty months of hostilities.

The Battle of New Orleans had nothing to do with the outcome of the war—a peace treaty had been signed at Ghent in Belgium on December 24, 1814, more than two weeks before the battle was fought. But news of the victory at New Orleans reached the American people before they learned of the peace treaty. The popular perception was that the battle had decided the outcome of the war. Andrew Jackson became an instant military hero and was on his way to the presidency of the United States. ➤

◄ *Andrew Jackson first came to Florida in 1814 following his victory over the Red Stick Creeks at the Battle of Horseshoe Bend. He proceeded to Pensacola, where he expelled the British. In 1818, Jackson returned to Pensacola. Governor José Masot surrendered, but Jackson withdrew five days later. Refusing to punish Jackson, President Monroe did agree to return the territory to Spain. After Florida became U.S. property, Jackson was dispatched to Pensacola to handle the transfer of Florida from Spain to the United States. Jackson appointed his cronies as officials and infuriated the Spanish government by imprisoning José Callava, the former governor of Florida. Jackson left Pensacola in October 1821, leaving behind many political colleagues who continued to dominate the area long after it became official U.S. territory. (Historical Association of Southern Florida)*

Negro Abraham.

▲ *Escaped slaves found sanctuary among the Seminoles and constituted important members of their society. This is the black Seminole Abraham. (Historical Association of Southern Florida)*

◀ *Gregor MacGregor, a Scottish adventurer and one of Simón Bolívar's most valuable lieutenants, landed at Fernandina on June 29, 1817. Seizing the Spanish garrison, MacGregor held the fort until money and supplies furnished by American merchants ran out. Aid that never materialized forced MacGregor to abandon the region, and the expedition soon ended in failure. (Florida State Archives)*

▼ *The old Spanish jail where Jackson ordered Spanish Governor Callava imprisoned because of his refusal to hand over papers concerning the estate of Nicholas Maria Vidal, a Spanish military official who had been dead for fifteen years. Drawing by Pensacola resident Emma Chandler. (Pensacola Historical Society)*

The Negro Fort

Governor Kindelán had been correct in his belief that the United States would take umbrage at Colonel Nicholls's actions in West Florida. Before withdrawing, Nicholls left a large number of blacks with a well-defended fort at Prospect Bluff on the Apalachicola River. Some Georgia planters believed that raids to free their slaves were being conducted from this so-called Negro Fort. As the Georgians increased their complaints that their slaves were being driven off by the marauders, the Spanish governor admitted his inability to cope with the Seminoles and blacks in his domain.

To deal with the situation, General Edmund P. Gaines built Fort Scott on the Flint River in extreme southwest Georgia, intending to supply it through Spanish Florida. He was not concerned with the violation of Spanish borders, but he knew the Negro Fort would be a problem. A combined force of Lower Creeks and U.S. Army personnel sailed up the river in July 1816 and encountered fire from the fort. When they fired back, a lucky shot sent a hot cannonball into a powder magazine and blew the fort apart, killing 271 black occupants and wounding most of the 64 survivors.

Filibustering on Amelia Island

The American military presence at Fort Scott remained a problem, but matters in East Florida took precedence for a while. Claiming to be "Brigadier General of the Armies of the United Provinces of New Granada and Venezuela," and "General in Chief of the Supreme Government of Mexico and South America," General Gregor MacGregor, a Scottish soldier of fortune who had fought with Simón Bolívar in Venezuela, sailed into Fernandina in the summer of 1817 and took the fort from the Spaniards without firing a shot. The audacious filibusterer apparently had a commission from the governments named, but it had been signed in Philadelphia in March of that year. When it became clear that he did not have a force sufficient to take East Florida, MacGregor left Ruggles Hubbard, a former New York sheriff, and Jared Irwin, a former Pennsylvania congressman, in charge and set off to raise funds.

He was not long gone when Luis Aury, a former Mexican patriot turned pirate, sailed into Fernandina. After a brief period of uncertainty, Aury joined MacGregor's force, apparently with the approval of Irwin and Hubbard, took command of Amelia Island, and raised the flag of the Mexican Revolution. Within a short time, the island became a depot for handling the booty taken by buccaneers throughout the Caribbean, including a number of African slaves who were smuggled from there into the United States, where the foreign slave trade had been officially ended in 1808.

United States Occupation in Trust

Under orders from President James Monroe, Captain J. D. Henley led a naval force with army support to Fernandina. Protesting mightily, Aury withdrew. Secretary of State John Quincy Adams wrote the Spanish minister that the United States had occupied Amelia Island because of the past piratical activities and that it would hold the territory in trust until the Spanish government was able to retake control of it.

The First Seminole War

In early 1818 the simmering situation along the Apalachicola River boiled into what became known as the First Seminole War. The Monroe administration was negotiating with Spain for the cession of Florida, but it was decided that direct action was necessary immediately to deal with a rapidly deteriorating border situation. Georgia planters were pressing General Gaines to help them recover their runaway slaves, believed to be near Boleck's (Bowlegs) town on the Suwannee River. Alexander Arbuthnot, an Englishman who had a trading post at St. Marks, was suspected of encouraging Seminole hostilities along the border. Blaming the Spanish government for failing to control the border and for allowing men such as Arbuthnot to operate there, the United States once again ordered General Jackson into the field.

With about one thousand Tennessee militiamen, Jackson marched 450 miles in forty-six days and reached Fort Scott on March 19, 1818. He immediately set out along the Apalachicola River to meet a supply squadron on the coast. After being resupplied, Jackson marched back to Prospect Bluff where the Negro Fort had been and erected a temporary fort that he named Fort Gadsden in honor of Lieutenant James Gadsden, the young engineering officer who built it. From there, Jackson marched back to Fort Scott to meet a band of Creek allies commanded by General William McIntosh. Proceeding to a Miccosukee village on the shore of the lake by that name, he began a running skirmish with his Indian adversaries, who fled toward the protection of St. Marks or to Boleck's town more than a hundred miles south of the Spanish border.

Arriving at St. Marks, Jackson sent a note to the Spanish commander explaining that he intended to occupy the fort but that he would respect Spanish property and personnel and would withdraw as soon as he had dealt with the Seminoles and their black allies. The astounded Spanish official did not respond quickly enough, and the impetuous general took over the fort anyway. After arresting Arbuthnot, he struck out for Boleck's town. He found that place mostly deserted, but arrested Robert C. Ambrister, another British citizen, and two black companions whom he found there. He also found in Ambrister's possession a letter from Arbuthnot warning of Jackson's presence in Florida. The enraged general blamed Arbuthnot for his failure to engage the Seminoles. Returning to St. Marks, he hanged Arbuthnot, stood Ambrister before a firing squad, and also executed two Indian leaders.

The Adams-Onis Treaty

Responding to a report that a band of Seminoles was at Pensacola under protection of the Spanish garrison, Jackson rushed there and demanded entrance to the city. When the Spanish governor refused, Jackson captured Pensacola, and the so-called First Seminole War was over. By the spring of 1818, Jackson had attacked and scattered the Seminoles about one hundred miles inside Spanish territory, executed two British citizens, and briefly occupied two Spanish garrisons. An

THE CHANGE of FLAGS ~ JULY 10TH 1821

▲ *The official surrender of Spanish Florida to the United States in 1821. (St. Augustine Historical Society)*

The Adams-Onis Treaty and John C. Calhoun's Misfortune

When President James Monroe decided to support General Andrew Jackson's invasion of Florida and his executions of Arbuthnot and Ambrister, Jackson simply assumed that he received that support because his superior, Secretary of War John C. Calhoun, had defended him. The general did not learn differently for nearly thirteen years, and the timing was unfortunate for Calhoun.

In the early 1830s when Jackson was president and Calhoun was vice president, the younger man had good reason to believe that he would succeed Old Hickory as president. But the two had serious differences when Calhoun led his native South Carolina in attempting to resist national legislation in the name of states' rights.

While Jackson was fuming over Calhoun's role in the so-called nullification crisis, someone told him about the cabinet meeting back in 1818 when Calhoun had recommended censuring him while Secretary of State John Quincy Adams had defended him. The two men never spoke again. Jackson backed Martin Van Buren for president in 1836, and John C. Calhoun's name became best known in association with states' rights, nullification, secession, and the Civil War.

amazed President James Monroe met with his cabinet, some members of which wanted to punish the general. Secretary of State John Quincy Adams argued otherwise. Exasperated at Spanish vacillation over the impending cession treaty, Adams suggested that Jackson be supported as a warning to the Spanish that their options were to get out of Florida, control the border, or expect more of the same. The president agreed with Adams, and the Spanish saw the futility of remaining in Florida. Thus the Adams-Onis Treaty was completed on February 22, 1819, although other matters delayed ratification until 1821.

Andrew Jackson was named to receive the territory from Spain and to establish a territorial government. After a stormy transitional period during which Jackson briefly jailed Spanish Governor José Callava, the Spaniards departed, Florida was organized as a single territory, and Jackson left for Tennessee.

Chapter 5

A Florida Scout. 1836.

Frontier Entrepreneurs, Persistent Seminoles, and the Struggle for Statehood 1821–1845

◄ *A Florida scout during the Second Seminole War, 1836. (University of South Florida Library— Special Collection)*

▼ *John James Audubon painted this pelican near Pensacola in 1837. (Pace Library—University of West Florida)*

▲ *In 1835, famed artist George Catlin and his wife, Clara, visited his brother James of Pensacola. In his* Letters and Notes on the Manners, Customs and Conditions *of the North American Indians, Catlin included this painting of a Seminole family drying fish on Santa Rosa Island. Towering sand dunes lend an arctic appearance to the scene. (Smithsonian Institution—National Museum of American Art)*

◄ This brick waterfront home was built by George Barkley in 1835 for his wife Clara Garnier, a native of France, and their seven children. Located on Floridablanca Street, the home served as a center for Pensacola society. Opening a reading room specializing in commercial information, Barkley expanded his business to include a general mercantile firm. Considered a leading citizen of the community, Barkley advocated "promotion of public morals, the diffusion of education, and the relief and comfort of the poor and needy." (Pensacola Historical Society)

*S*everal hundred Americans and a few Spaniards, their land titles guaranteed by the cession treaty, made up the population of Florida when Andrew Jackson received it in the name of the United States. St. Augustine and Pensacola each hoped to become the seat of government now that East and West Florida had been united. Efforts to please both communities by alternating the legislative sessions proved impractical, however, and William H. Simmons and John Lee Williams were commissioned to find a suitable compromise location. Their choice of the site that became Tallahassee, roughly equidistant between the two older towns, brought the center of government to the hilly region that was soon being called Middle Florida. The selection of the Tallahassee site coincided with other events of the early 1820s to stimulate a land boom in the region between the Apalachicola and Suwannee rivers.

The third decade of the nineteenth century was a time of rapid expansion and expectant optimism in America. After surviving the War of 1812 without serious loss and having at least temporarily allayed sectional differences in what became known as the Era of Good Feeling, Americans began pushing westward and southward in search of land and the opportunity to develop it. From the tidewater area between Maryland and South Carolina, from New York, and from Georgia and Alabama came land-hungry settlers who had heard of the excellent lands in Middle Florida. There was reason for their optimism. The separation of their nation from the Old World by an ocean, and a broad, largely unpopulated continent before them, gave these expectant capitalists confidence in their abilities to make for themselves a life of substance and satisfaction.

An Incipient Cotton Kingdom

For those who moved southward, the avenue to success was cotton cultivation. Upland cotton became a potentially profitable crop after Eli Whitney demonstrated his cotton gin in 1793. The spread of that crop across the southeastern states coincided with the Industrial Revolution, which increased the demand for raw cotton. Andrew Jackson's defeat of the Creeks had opened millions of acres of land along the Georgia and Alabama borders, attracting many potential cotton planters. They soon discovered that the clay hills of Middle Florida were superior cotton lands.

Territorial Boosterism

Avid promoters such as Richard Keith Call were soon spreading the word. Having accompanied Andrew Jackson on the 1818 campaign, Call chose to remain in Florida. By the time he reached Washington as territorial representative in 1825, he was convinced of the future of the territory and eager to speed it along. His glowing reports convinced such dignitaries as John Branch, a future cabinet member and territorial governor; the Marquis de Lafayette, to whom a grateful United States granted a township of land which cornered in present-day Tallahassee; Prince Achille Murat, who had been at home in the capitals of Europe before becoming a thoroughgoing democrat on the Florida frontier; and William Wirt, the somewhat visionary attorney general of the United States during the Monroe and Adams administrations.

Prince Murat moved to Middle Florida in 1825, developed his Lipona plantation, married a descendant of George Washington, and became a highly regarded neighbor to the entrepreneurial planters who were pouring into the region. His

Frontier Diplomacy

Perhaps no titled European ever accommodated to the frontier so thoroughly or enjoyed it so much as Prince Achille Murat. After circulating in the courts of Europe with all their pomp and circumstance, he was duly impressed with the much simpler methods of territorial Florida. When Governor Duval and James Gadsden were preparing for the meeting with the Seminoles that resulted in the 1828 Treaty of Payne's Landing, Murat witnessed a meeting between the governor and Gadsden at the latter's cabin.

The prince was amazed and delighted at the arrival of the territorial governor, clad in buckskins and Indian moccasins and dismounting a bony horse. The governor then entered the cabin, where he and his "chief emissary" to the tribal chiefs sat on a dirt floor eating dried meat with their fingers and drinking whiskey from a jug while they discussed high matters of state. When the conference was finished, the governor rolled up in a bearskin and slept on the floor. That was hardly the way official proceedings were carried out in the courts of Europe! ➤

business partner was James Gadsden, another soldier who had accompanied Jackson in 1818, and remained in Florida to seek his fortune.

At Call's urging, William Wirt became one of Middle Florida's strongest promoters. In a day when "conflict of interest" was not yet a part of our political vocabulary, some Floridians thought the acquisition of such a distinguished citizen as the U.S. attorney general would be an asset and assisted him in making prudent purchases. Both Call and Governor William P. Duval used their knowledge of the local land market as well as their official positions to help Wirt procure desirable parcels. By 1827 Wirt owned several large tracts in the Middle Florida cotton belt. He was still planning to move there when he died in 1834, but his widow, three sons, and four daughters lived in Florida at various times, and one daughter and one son are buried there. His Wirtland plantation became a showplace for many years and is still a familiar landmark in Jefferson County.

Agricultural Entrepreneurs

It was Call and Wirt who brought the possibilities of Middle Florida to the attention of John and Robert Gamble. From a Virginia family long interested in both planting and transportation, the Gamble brothers were typical of the many younger members of established families who sought their fortunes in the new land. The two men gathered their families and their slaves and set out in a wagon train for Florida in early 1826. After a journey of several weeks, they were clearing land in Jefferson County by midsummer.

Robert's Welaunee and John's Waukeenah plantations covered roughly 10,000 acres. Intending at first to grow sugar cane, they found the growing season too short and took up cotton cultivation instead. The brothers each acquired over one

---

The Code Duello

Dueling was against the law in territorial Florida but was still accepted by custom. Gentlemen who believed their honor besmirched would often challenge their adversaries to duels, and their rivals considered themselves honor-bound to accept. An accident of history provided a suitable solution to the disparity between law and custom.

While running the boundary line between U.S. and Spanish possessions in 1800, Andrew Ellicott had surveyed from west to east. When he attempted to cross the Apalachicola River, he met fierce resistance from the Seminoles then living in the area. Ellicott abandoned his eastward trek and went downriver to the Gulf and around the peninsula to the St. Marys River. He then went upriver until he found a site that became known as Ellicott's Mound and drew the boundary according to measurements from that point. Unfortunately, Ellicott's Mound was subsequently confused with another point of high ground, and future maps showed variations in the border.

For many years a "no man's land" existed between that which was certainly Georgia and that which was unquestionably Florida. It caused headaches for tax collectors in both states for many decades, and the last vestiges of the dispute were not finally settled until an agreement was signed in 1967 by Lester Maddox of Georgia and Claude Kirk of Florida. But during the antebellum years, the disputed area provided a dueling ground where Floridians could practice their code of honor without running afoul of the laws that they themselves had enacted to prevent this customary handling of disagreements between gentlemen. ➤

TO THE PUBLIC.

The object of this placard is to inform the Public that Gen. Leigh Read has declined giving to me an apology for the insult offered me at St. Marks, on the 5th inst. That he has also refused to me that satisfaction, which as an honorable man, (refusing to apologise.) he was bound to give. I therefore pronounce him a Coward and a Scoundrel.
WILLIAM TRADEWELL.
Tallahassee. Oct. 26, 1839.

▲ *A duel placard posted in a public area of Tallahassee in 1839. Whether arising from aristocratic pretensions or from a lack of institutionalized law, dueling became a part of the South's code of honor. (Florida State Archives)*

hundred slaves and were soon farming large acreages and hauling their cotton by wagon to port, first to Magnolia and later to Newport. After becoming president of the Union Bank of Tallahassee, John purchased and moved to his Neamathla plantation closer to the capital city while he continued to operate his Waukeenah plantation. The brothers and their descendants became influential in the political, social, and economic affairs of the territory.

In 1825 the Florida territory contained about 13,000 inhabitants with fewer than 2,500 living between the Apalachicola and the Suwannee rivers. Fifteen years later, there were 54,500 Floridians, 34,000 of whom were living in Middle Florida. It was cotton production from large plantations using slave labor that accounted for the population boom, but there were many obstacles that had first to be overcome.

But for a Suitable Port

John and Nathaniel Hamlin were from Maine, sons of a Yankee trader who had bought and sold goods at St. Marks. Recognizing the possibilities of middle Florida, they laid out and built the town of Magnolia on the upper St. Marks River. It was not a good site: the river was shallow and narrow, and even smaller vessels usually had to descend the river backwards because there was no way to turn around. But the town was near the developing plantations and optimism ran high. The Hamlins opened their factorage in 1827, and by the following year Edward Seixas, Benjamin Bird, William L. Haskins, and several others were buying cotton for shipment and selling plantation supplies. Some of them owned their own ships for the cotton trade. The most ambitious project was probably the Merchants and Planters Bank, which opened in 1832. A brisk competition with the older port of St. Marks developed.

Magnolia reached its zenith about 1833 and began declining. The river was simply too shallow, despite enthusiastic booster claims. Tallahassee became a serious competitor when its muledrawn railroad to St. Marks opened in 1835. The deathblow came in 1835 when the United States Supreme Court nullified the Hamlins' title to the Magnolia town site. The old Forbes grant by which the Indians had paid their debts to the Panton, Leslie Company was acquired by Colin Mitchel. While the U.S. land office was busily disposing of the land to settlers, Mitchel was in court seeking title to his land. In 1835, the courts agreed with Mitchel, and Magnolia died within months. The Hamlins and other factors moved to the new town of Port Leon. Downriver toward Apalachee Bay with much deeper water and served by the Tallahassee Railroad, it became the outlet for Middle Florida cotton until 1843, when a devastating hurricane demonstrated the difficulties of deep water and a low shoreline.

As the hurricane waters receded, the Port Leon merchants met in one of the few remaining buildings and named a committee to find a compromise location between the shallow waters of Magnolia and the dangerous coast of Port Leon. They chose a site on the St. Marks River, where a new town appropriately named Newport was laid out, a bridge across the river was completed, and merchants were shipping cotton within weeks after the disastrous hurricane. In the meantime other problems beset the Middle Florida planting community.

◀ *The Magnolia plantation at St. Marks, 1842. Lithograph by French artist A. Bertrand. (Florida State Archives)*

◀ *Neamathla, the great chief of the Miccosukees, as depicted in 1838. He foresaw grief in the relocation of Seminole tribes from their north Florida homes to the sandy and barren lands farther south. (University of South Florida Library—Special Collection)*

The Seminoles Again

The several Indian bands that collectively became known as the Seminoles had been drifting into Florida since the 1750s to escape the pressures of the white man's advancing frontier. The latest addition was the Red Stick Creeks, who had lost their land in Alabama and Georgia in the Treaty of Fort Jackson. They and their neighbors must have been dismayed by the rush of whites into northern Florida in the early 1820s. Living in scattered villages across the same red hills that were attracting white settlers, the Indians frequently encountered their new neighbors. Tiger Tail of the Tallahassee band was a frequent visitor at Robert Gamble's Welaunee plantation. The main east-west trail used by the Indians ran less than a mile south of Waukeenah.

White settlers often bought venison, nuts, and sweet potatoes from the natives. But there were also unfriendly encounters. There was a fundamental conflict between the new, sedentary agriculturalists with their specific ideas of private property ownership and their advanced political organization and a seminomadic hunting and pastoral people who viewed the land as a common possession and whose governing system was fragmented and localized. The difficulties arising in Middle Florida were part of a general pattern across the southeast United States that was creating a clamor for removal of the Indians.

As ex-officio Indian agent, Governor Duval, joined by James Gadsden and Bernard Segui, first attempted to relocate the Indians. According to the 1823 Treaty of Fort Moultrie, most of the Seminoles ostensibly agreed to move to a four-million-acre tract in the central peninsula in return for supplies, some technical assistance, and a small annuity. Regarding the treaty, Andrew Jackson declared that he had "no hesitation in saying the government will experience some

▲ *George Catlin's painting of Osceola is regarded by many as a classic expression of courage and dignity. (Smithsonian Institution—National Museum of American Art)*

difficulty in concentrating the Florida Indians . . . in the peninsula." His prediction proved to be correct, if somewhat understated.

Some of the Indians were not required to move, others who were expected to do so never did, and still others went to the reservation and soon left it because it was an unsatisfactory place for them to maintain their accustomed livelihood. Without a place to live acceptable to the whites, the returning bands roamed among the white settlers and confrontations were frequent. Individuals from both sides committed violent acts. The chiefs tried to cooperate with white authorities, but justice was always one-sided. Governor Duval said he "felt ashamed while urging the Indians to surrender the property they hold, that I had not power to obtain for them their own rights. . . . To tell one of these people that he must go to law for his property, in our courts, with a white man is only adding insult to injury."

Removal to the West

By the time Andrew Jackson became president in 1829, the demand for removal of the Indians to a western territory was loud and strident. Jackson was receptive to the idea. Although the Seminoles believed that the Treaty of Fort Moultrie gave them the right to remain in Florida for twenty years, many of them were near starvation by the early 1830s when the government began negotiating with them to leave. At a meeting with James Gadsden, some of the chiefs agreed to go to Indian Territory to investigate its suitability for their relocation. At Fort Gibson in that territory, they signed an agreement to move, but upon their return to Florida they were denounced and ridiculed by a group of younger Seminoles led by Osceola and Coacoochee. All of the signers except one repudiated the treaty; the lone holdout was ambushed and killed while leading his band toward Fort Brooke on Tampa Bay, where ships were waiting to take him to Oklahoma.

The Second Seminole War

General Wiley Thompson, who had recently become commissioner in charge of removal of the Seminoles, inherited the relocation problem. At his Fort King headquarters near Ocala, eight chiefs agreed to take their people west, but Micanopy, Jumper, Alligator, Black Dirt, and Arpeika refused. Angered by their defiance, Thompson summarily deposed the proud Indians as chiefs. When his superiors in Washington overruled him, Thompson agreed to another meeting. At this gathering he quarreled with Osceola and threw him in jail. He erred grievously by letting him out after several days of detention. During the next several weeks, the U.S. authorities prepared for removal while most of the Indians were gradually deciding to resist. On December 28, 1835, Thompson strolled outside the fort with a friend late in the evening. Both were killed by a volley fired from ambush by Osceola and his accomplices. On the same day, Major Francis Dade and a column of troops on their way from Fort Brooke to Fort King were ambushed and annihilated by Indians led by Micanopy, Alligator, and Coacoochee. The Second Seminole War had begun.

During the next several years, Indian depredations severely damaged the Florida economy. The sugar plantations in Mosquito County (now Volusia) were deci-

◀ An 1852 illustration of Billy Bowlegs and his chiefs. Left to right: Billy Bowlegs, Chocote Tustenuggee, Abraham, John Jumper, Fasatchee Emanthla, and Sarparkee Yohola. (University of South Florida Library—Special Collection)

◀ Seminole war veteran Thia-thlo-tutenukka, also known as Old Man Fish, sat for this portrait in the mid-1800s. (Historical Association of Southern Florida)

▼ With white settlers spreading into all areas of the South, Florida's Seminoles fought for their lands. After three long and expensive wars, U.S. officials rounded up and banished many of the Seminoles to the western Indian Territory. The few remaining Seminoles escaped into the swamps, with most fleeing to the Everglades. (Historical Association of Southern Florida)

SORROWS OF THE SEMINOLES—BANISHED FROM FLORIDA.

mated and nearly all the settlers fled. The growing community of Jacksonville was threatened by Indian raids. The Middle Florida plantations were repeatedly attacked and numerous casualties were reported. One sea captain swore never to return to Florida after his vessel was attacked while backing down the river from Magnolia with a load of cotton. With their knowledge of the terrain, the Indians fought a successful guerrilla war using tactics unfamiliar to the regular United States Army.

Nothing but an Indian in Every Bush

As commander of the Florida militia, General Richard Keith Call fought an inconclusive battle with the Seminoles at the Withlacoochee River in early 1836, but General Winfield Scott arrived soon afterward to take the field with regular troops. When the general took his 6,000-man army into summer quarters rather than pursue the Indians, he was burned in effigy by a crowd in Tallahassee. The angry Scott denounced "the good people of several large districts" who could see "nothing but an Indian in every bush" and "fled without knowing whether they ran from Squaws or Warriors." The furious Floridians had long memories, and when Scott ran for president in 1852, they rushed to the polls and gleefully voted for his opponent.

Treachery or Astute Diplomacy?

Thomas S. Jesup succeeded Scott and launched an apparently successful sweep of the central peninsula. Several chiefs soon expressed willingness to take their people to Fort Brooke, but when interminable delays followed, the general became suspicious of their intent. Apparently believing that the Indians were deceiving him, Jesup evidently felt justified in arresting Osceola, Coacoochee, and several others under a flag of truce in early 1837. He was embarrassed when Coacoochee escaped from Fort Marion and quickly spread the word of the general's treachery among his allies.

A War without Victor

Jesup was shortly replaced by Zachary Taylor, who fought Coacoochee at

Okeechobee, the largest single battle of the war and one that inflicted significant damage on the Indians. That was the last pitched battle of the Second Seminole War, although hostilities continued for nearly four more years. By 1841, warfare had decimated the Indian population and its economic situation was desperate. Many bands gave up and went to Tampa for transportation westward. After inducing Coacoochee to help round up most of the remaining Indians, Colonel William J. Worth in 1842 asked for and received permission to allow the handful of holdouts to stay in Florida. The United States declared the war over. To the few remaining Seminoles, now deep in the Everglades, it mattered little.

No Surplus Capital

Optimism was still running high in the early 1830s, and the Middle Florida planters were eager to expand their holdings and increase production. But like all inhabitants of the rapidly growing frontiers of the time, they found investment capital exceedingly scarce. John Gamble and some of his neighbors began urging the charter of banks through which capital might be raised. He and other planters and merchants opened the Merchants and Planters Bank at Magnolia and the Central Bank of Florida, of which he became president. These and a few other banks were, however, unable to provide the resources considered necessary, and the capital-hungry Floridians sought other ways of supplying the money they needed.

The answer seemed to lie in a cooperative arrangement between the government and its citizens. The legislative council chartered three banks to operate on that premise, the most important of which was the Union Bank of Tallahassee. That bank was permitted to issue stock to be paid for with mortgages on land, slaves, or any revenue-yielding property. The bank needed operating cash to make loans and carry out general banking business, but because stock issues paid for by mortgages did not create cash, the legislative council was to step in and assist.

Snead's Smokehouse

Although they probably would never notice it, travelers along a two-lane road in northeastern Jefferson County might be surprised to learn that one of the beautiful ponds they pass was once known as Snead's Smokehouse. It is a venerable appellation stemming from ante-bellum plantation days and the economic and social customs relating to slavery.

One of the most important edifices on the early plantations was the smokehouse. A large overhead cost of keeping slaves to work the fields was incurred in providing adequate food, and it was from that lowly outbuilding that meat and staples were dispensed. It was obviously in the best economic interest of the planter to provide an adequate diet for his work force, and it was almost equally important to avoid acquiring a reputation for mistreatment.

At the same time, there were many ways of cutting the outlay for meat and staples. Several overseers of the region were proud that they provided part of their plantation's meat supply from their successful hunting. According to stories that still circulate in Jefferson County, Anderson Snead had another source of supply. Although he was a member in good standing of plantation society, he gained an enduring reputation for sending his slaves to the lake to catch fish instead of giving them a regular meat ration from his smokehouse. ➤

The governor was authorized to issue six-percent bonds maturing in thirty years and to pledge the faith of the territory as security. By 1838, more than $3 million in "faith bonds" had been issued and sold to European investors on the strength of the official endorsement. The Union Bank also had power to issue currency that could be loaned on mortgage security. Stockholders could receive loans for up to two-thirds of the value of their original investments through long-term mortgages of their land and slaves.

According to these generous provisions, the Union Bank opened for business with its capital assets mostly in land and slaves. It sold bonds backed by the territorial government to raise cash and loaned the proceeds to planters, many of whom were shareholders, on mortgages of more land and slaves. It was a pyramidal scheme that might have worked if the economy had continued to grow, but that was not to be. The deflationary stresses following the national panic of 1837 and lasting until about 1842 were disastrous to this ill-advised policy.

The Union Bank was obliged to suspend specie payment in the late 1830s, and John Gamble spent the last years of his life liquidating the bank's assets. In 1842, a distressed legislative council repudiated the bonds it had issued in support of the bank. The national depression and the disastrous Indian war were accompanied by natural disasters. The worst drought on record decimated the Middle Florida crops in 1839, then a yellow fever epidemic swept the area in 1841. A huge destructive storm in 1842 was followed by a much greater one in 1843; the latter storm completely destroyed Port Leon. The final crushing blow was a long-lasting drop in cotton prices in the early 1840s.

Covered with Judgments

Realizing that its only chance for survival was the ability of its debtors to continue in business, the Union Bank was most reluctant to foreclose on its loans. It was soon obliged, however, to enter suits to protect its investors. Individuals began suing each other in forlorn hopes of survival, and the bank was forced to follow suit. One observer declared that Middle Florida was "covered with judgments." By the time Florida became a state in 1845, there were no banks operating there. Planters were still trying to sort out their debts and assets and continue to plant. Some lost out and went elsewhere, most were less optimistic and more realistic than they had been in the halcyon days of the 1820s, but many remained and helped to build the new state of Florida.

One State or Two?

Despite Indian wars, depression, and low cotton prices, the territory continued to grow during the 1830s. Talk of statehood increased, with supporters touting the opportunity to elect their officials instead of having to rely on presidential appointments. But residents of east Florida disagreed. Because they lived in a poor, sparsely settled region that had been devastated by the Indian raids, these settlers argued that statehood would require more taxes than they could afford to pay. Their solution was to divide the Florida territory along the Suwannee River and allow the eastern portion to maintain its territorial status.

Despite this disagreement, a constitutional convention was approved, which in

▲ *After the United States gained possession of Florida, a French visitor sketched the Chattahoochee Mt. Vernon arsenal, c. 1839. The old fort tower stands in the center; parts of it remain today as the Drink Stand Building. (Library of Congress)*

Before There Was Federal Disaster Relief

Having had to relocate their port from Magnolia, where the water was too shallow, to Port Leon, where the land was too low, the merchants on Apalachee Bay might have had good reason to call for assistance when their town was destroyed by a ten-foot wall of water in September 1843. Instead of seeking governmental assistance as has become customary today, the hardy merchants met in what remained of the Port Leon Hotel and named a committee to seek a better site. Within two days the committee had decided that the best alternative was at what became Newport, close enough to the coast for adequate water in the river and far enough inland to give some protection from future tidal waves. While one committee laid out a town site and sold lots, another contracted for a bridge to be built across the river to facilitate freight from the east.

The storm had destroyed Port Leon on September 13, 1843. On October 17 the brig *R. W. Brown* arrived at the new town of Newport to load cotton that was already waiting on the wharves.

1838 drafted a document that the people approved by a narrow majority. By that time Florida was developing as a typical Southern state with an agricultural economy based on slave labor. Since the Missouri Compromise of 1821, Congress had maintained a balance between free and slave states by admitting one of each when there were admissions. Florida's admission was delayed for several years because of the sectional dispute within the territory and because there was no corresponding free territory prepared for statehood. By 1845, however, Iowa had applied for admission. Over the continued opposition of east Floridians, Florida was admitted to the Union on March 3, 1845.

Most white Floridians in 1845 were small landowners who lived and worked on subsistence farms. But despite their minority status, the planters produced the vast majority of the crops that were exported and slaves did most of the work on their lands. These planters were the political, economic, and social leaders of the new state. Floridians had worked hard to earn the right of statehood, but they joined the Union just as their way of life was becoming a matter of controversy in the nation, and in a few short years many Floridians would be working just as diligently to leave it.

Chapter 6

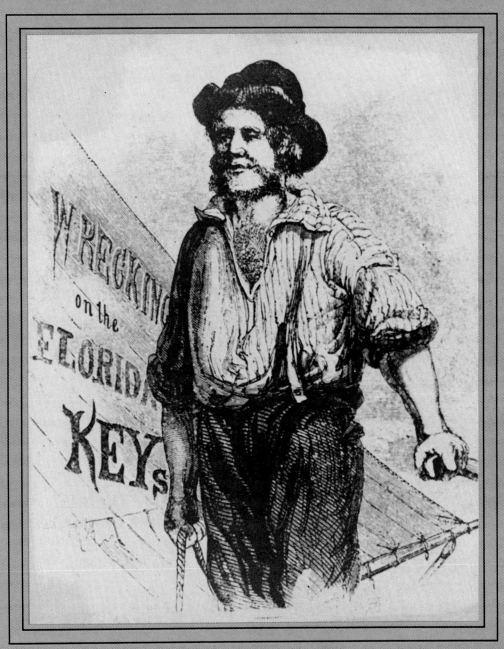

From Statehood
to Secession
1845–1861

T. 76

Ardea cærulea

◄*A Key West wrecker in the early 1800s. Salvaging was one of the town's earliest and most profitable industries. Wreckers would* lie in wait for a vessel in distress, salvage the cargo, and sell it for a tidy profit. *(Monroe County Library)*

▲*The blue heron, from Mark Catesby's* Natural History of Carolina, Florida and the Bahama Islands. *(University of South Florida—Special Collection)*

◀ *Angela Moreno Mallory, daughter of a Spanish patriarch, married Stephen Mallory of Pensacola, who served as a U.S. senator and later as the Confederacy's secretary of the navy. During her husband's political career, which covered a period of 15 years, Angela carried the burdens of parenting and domestic responsibilities alone. (Pensacola Historical Society)*

*T*he new state was still struggling with the aftermath of the recent depression when cheering crowds celebrated William Moseley's inauguration as Florida's first governor in 1845. Many Floridians struggled with debt for years and John Gamble spent the remaining seven years of his life settling the affairs of the failed Union Bank, but gradually there were signs of improvement. The new state remained without banks, but the cotton factors developed a credit system that enabled them and their planting customers to conduct business on an annual basis, settling their accounts each year when the crops were sold. This credit system worked well enough in the absence of adequate circulating medium. Newport, Tallahassee, and St. Marks continued to handle most of the cotton and other products of Middle Florida and to supply the needs of the plantations. With forty-six factors and a river system extending to Columbus, Georgia, Apalachicola became the third largest port on the Gulf by the mid-1850s. As cotton prices rose in the late 1840s, Florida entered a period of general prosperity.

Settlements on the Manatee

Some planters had not waited for the return of cotton profits. Having learned more about peninsular Florida during the Indian war and spurred by the Armed Occupation Act that offered free land to people wishing to move into the uninhabited region, Joseph and Hector Braden, some of the Gambles, and a few others moved to the Manatee River country and began growing sugar cane. While profits eluded them in that volatile industry, their plantations formed the nucleus of the later settlements of Bradenton and Sarasota.

The Rising Lumber Industry

While the plantations were recovering, lumber was giving rise to new entrepreneurs and new towns. Pensacola enjoyed a revival as schooners from the northeastern United States and Europe began carrying yellow pine from west Florida mills. By the late 1840s, lumber from that port was being shipped to the northeastern states, to England and western Europe, and to Cuba, Brazil, and other Latin American destinations. But it was Jacksonville that owed its rise as a major ante-bellum port town to lumber. Known as Cowford until the 1820s and chartered in 1832, it served as an army supply depot and a target of Seminole raiding parties in the mid-1830s before becoming a thriving lumber port. Since live oak and pine had been cut along the St. Johns River and shipped abroad for decades before the United States acquired Florida, it was perhaps natural that Jacksonville became the site of sawmills as interest in Florida's yellow pine increased.

The Key of the Gulf

As the port of entry for commerce entering the Gulf and a stopover for vessels engaged in the coasting trade from Maine to Texas, Key West became the most populous town in Florida, a distinction it retained for nearly a half-century. But even as the island community was achieving prominence based on water transportation, Key West's future was being undercut by the innovation of railway transport. Until the early nineteenth century, oceans had been the highways of travel and rivers the secondary roads; canals supplemented the rivers. As the technol-

▲ *The Gamble mansion in Ellenton, built between 1845 and 1850, as it appeared in 1902. Once the center of a 3,500-acre plantation with 1,500 acres in sugar cane, the mansion symbolized both the beauty of the Old South and its post–Civil War ruin. The restored structure is now maintained by the state of Florida. (Florida State Archives)*

The Ice Man

Ice was a scarce commodity in ante-bellum Florida. It was sometimes available at prices ranging from three to fifty cents per pound, but it was not always there when it was needed. That was the case in 1850 when Monsieur Rosan, a cultivated native of France and a cotton factor at Apalachicola, planned his Bastille Day party. The ice ship was late, and it was a matter of much conjecture whether the Frenchman would be able to cool his champagne as promised. But he wagered that the ice would be there and that it would be produced locally. To the amazement of his guests, Dr. John Gorrie arrived at the appointed time with the ice. The host collected his bets and entertained in lavish style.

Dr. Gorrie, long concerned about the discomfort of his yellow fever patients, had been experimenting with ways to cool their hospital rooms. He had developed a system of refrigeration with which he cooled two of the rooms in his hospital and had accidentally discovered how to make ice. The demonstration at the Bastille Day party was the introduction of Gorrie's ice machine. During the next decade he tried unsuccessfully to obtain financing with which to develop and market his machine.

Ice was subsequently produced on a commercial scale in Europe and elsewhere and air conditioning eventually became common. Modern Florida depends heavily on both and they were introduced to the state from elsewhere, but artificial cooling happened first in Florida.

ogy became available, railroads slowly began replacing the water routes. Eventually, a network of railroads tied the nation together and drew its trade and travel inward, leaving Key West and some of the other ports in the backwater. While that process required time and the inevitable decline of the water routes became apparent only in retrospect, the rise of Jacksonville as a port town coincided with a growing interest among Floridians in railroad construction.

Early Railroad Schemes

Richard Keith Call and his Whig associates had built the primitive Tallahassee Railroad to St. Marks in the 1830s, and they took the lead in promoting a line that might connect the Gulf region to the Atlantic port of Savannah, or perhaps Charleston. Jacksonville boosters recognized early on the advantages of location that could transform their town into a transportation hub for the state. Although fierce competition would subsequently develop between the boosters of Savannah and those of Jacksonville, it was a political opponent of Call's and a promoter of Fernandina who seized the initiative in Florida's railroad development.

David Levy Yulee, a native of St. Thomas who had studied law in St. Augustine before becoming Florida's territorial delegate, had been instrumental in the statehood movement. Elected to the U.S. Senate by the first legislature, he soon turned his considerable energies to the development of a transportation system that would improve access to markets for Florida products and provide a means by which settlers could reach the vast vacant areas of the peninsula.

In the Public Interest

Recognizing that capital for railroad construction was scarce and profits would depend on growth, Yulee and other railroad advocates reasoned that the state's resources might be used in building lines and that the state would ultimately benefit from the resulting growth. They were delighted by the law enacted by Congress in 1850 that granted swamp and overflowed lands to the states in which they lay for drainage and reclamation. Florida thus acquired about ten million acres, and Yulee urged state leaders to use the acquisition to encourage railroad construction. Between 1851 and 1855, the legislature created the Internal Improvement Board and empowered it to use the land to assist private companies in constructing railroads from Jacksonville to Pensacola and from Fernandina to Tampa. Not only could the board grant large acreages to the companies for each mile of railway built, but it could also lend the credit of the state to help them sell their bonds to pay construction costs.

During the same period, the legislature chartered corporations to begin construction of those routes. The Florida Railroad Company, with David Yulee as president, was authorized to build a railway from Fernandina to Tampa with the privilege of extending a branch to Cedar Key. The Florida, Atlantic, and Gulf Central Railroad, whose president was Dr. Abel Baldwin, was permitted to build a line from Jacksonville to Lake City to connect with the Pensacola and Georgia Railroad, which would extend westward to Quincy.

With the state's financial backing and the prospect of thousands of acres of lands to be acquired by the successful companies, an enthusiastic public lent its support to the prospective rail lines. Counties and towns along the proposed routes subscribed substantial sums for construction in hopes of obtaining better transportation. By 1860 all of these roads and a short line from Pensacola to the Alabama border had been completed. They seemed destined to bind together the settled part of the state and to make the upper peninsula more accessible to settlers, but the Civil War intervened just as construction was completed and the railroad companies were left with huge debts and no revenues.

Of the Mind and Spirit

The railroad enthusiasm, the comparative prosperity of the Middle Florida cotton growers, and at least a measure of diversification through the growing timber industry offered a semblance of permanence to the Florida economy of the 1850s. There were signs of social advancement as well. In the early 1850's, the legislature enacted laws calling for public educational institutions, and many of the local communities were establishing creditable academies. Church congregations were building durable edifices, adding measurably to the physical appearances of the communities even as they served more spiritual needs. Many of the more successful planters preferred to live in town and leave the daily operation of their plantations to overseers. Some of them erected large and commodious homes that further enhanced the sense of stability and permanence. But there were contradictory trends as well.

Half Slave and Half Free

When Harriet Beecher Stowe's *Uncle Tom's Cabin* appeared in 1852, it exacerbated an already heated national debate over the existence of slavery in the southeastern states. Although the book was suppressed in Florida, it symbolized to many who never saw it the greatest single threat to the permanence of the society they were so busily building. Most white slave owners in Florida regarded the institution as essential to their economic well-being and as a suitable arrangement by which blacks and whites could live together in peace; moreover, they regarded themselves as humane masters who cared well for their chattel. Examples of excellent relations between white owners and black bondsmen are indeed as numerous as instances of physical abuse and degradation. But the slave owners never understood that such comparisons were irrelevant. Opponents of slavery charged that the institution was condemned by the promises inherent in the Declaration of Independence.

The Mexican War and Slavery in the Territories

When Floridians enthusiastically volunteered for service in the Mexican War, they did so as patriots eager to serve their country, but the outcome of the conflict unsettled the balance between the free and slave sections of the United States. Shortly after the Mexicans ceded the southwest to the United States, gold was discovered in California and the people there were soon clamoring for statehood. Admission of California as a free state threatened the balance that had existed since the Missouri Compromise, and Southerners balked at the prospect. David Yulee joined the radicals who called for secession from the Union. Sentiment for

▲ *The American rattlesnake, from Mark Catesby's* Natural History of Carolina, Florida and the Bahama Islands. *(University of South Florida—Special Collection)*

▲ Billy Bowlegs, chief of the Seminoles and defiant leader of the Third Seminole War. While cotton was king in north Florida and the nation was divided over slavery, Bowlegs was one of the Seminole chiefs who escaped to the Everglades rather than relocate to Oklahoma. (Florida Historical Society)

such action gradually subsided, and the fragile Compromise of 1850 was ultimately arranged. Its fragility was emphasized by the angry outcries provoked by the publication of *Uncle Tom's Cabin* barely two years later.

The South Carolina School

Almost as deeply embedded in the Southern psyche as the belief in the legitimacy of the slave system was the view that the states had sovereign rights which transcended the powers of the national government. John C. Calhoun of South Carolina had provided the philosophical basis for that belief, and it was widely accepted by Southerners in the 1850s. They believed that "domestic institutions" such as slavery were the responsibility of the individual states and that the national government should have no control over them.

These sentiments began to influence party politics in Florida just as partisan alignments were becoming significant in the new state. While the national Democratic party was attempting to maintain a moderate position on the slavery issue, the Florida Democrats were becoming much more radical. Numerous immigrants from South Carolina had settled in Alachua and Marion counties since the late 1840s, and they brought with them a strong belief in states' rights. This so-called South Carolina School, headed especially by James E. Broome and Madison S. Perry, gained rapid ascendance in the Florida Democratic party.

A Delayed Retribution

While the national Whigs generally tried to avoid the slavery question, the Northern wing of that party was becoming more antislavery. When the Whigs nominated Winfield Scott for president in 1852, they hoped that his military record would overshadow the more volatile question. Scott dashed that hope when

---

Caroline Lee Whiting Hentz and Harriet Beecher Stowe

Caroline Hentz was one of Florida's best-known ante-bellum authors. A Massachusetts native, she came to Florida by way of Cincinnati, Ohio, and Columbus, Georgia, where she and her husband operated schools for young women. When her husband became unable to work in the 1840s, she earned a living by producing a remarkable collection of novels and short stories. She is best known in Florida for her *Marcus Warland, or The Long Moss Spring* and *Eoline, or Magnolia Vale*, both published in 1852 and depicting plantation life in idyllic terms. More interesting to the historian is her less-known *Planter's Northern Bride*.

Having known Harriet Beecher Stowe when the two belonged to the same literary club in Cincinnati, Mrs. Hentz was dismayed when *Uncle Tom's Cabin* catalyzed antislavery opinion in the nation and around the world. Distressed over the growing enmity between her native state and the South that she had come to love, she went into seclusion and attempted to rebut Mrs. Stowe with *Planter's Northern Bride*, which portrayed slavery as a beneficent social arrangement. Her book appealed to Southerners, but it never had the influence of Stowe's sensational novel—which was probably the most despised book *never* read in the South. Both Mrs. Hentz and her husband died before the Civil War broke out, but two of her sons lived out their lives as medical doctors in Marianna and Quincy. ➤

▲ *A view of the Pensa-*
cola shipping docks in
the 1800s. (Florida
State Archives)

he announced his vigorous opposition to slavery. While Floridians probably voted against him as much for his insulting comments about their courage during the Indian War as for his antislavery views, Scott was rejected by both state and nation in favor of Democrat Franklin Pierce. More important for Floridians, however, was the election of James E. Broome as governor. From his inauguration in 1853, the "South Carolina School" held a dominant role in the Democratic party and the state.

The Kansas-Nebraska Act, "Bleeding Kansas," and John Brown

When Congress enacted the Kansas-Nebraska Act in 1854, it ostensibly opened to slavery territory that had barred the institution since the Missouri Compromise of 1821. Although there was little likelihood that slave owners would settle Kansas on the basis of plantation cotton agriculture, antislavery advocates were strongly opposed to the act. They disliked its theoretical alterations of the dividing line between slave and free territories, while Southerners favored it for the same reason. Unable to unite its disparate Northern and Southern wings after the act passed, the Whig party disintegrated. Meanwhile, the Northern wing of the Democratic party was weakened by the exodus of antislavery members and the Southern wing was commensurately strengthened. When the Republican party emerged almost spontaneously as a Northern party, the nation was effectively divided by both party and geography.

With both antislavery and proslavery settlers attempting to establish residence in Kansas, Henry Titus, founder of Titusville, and other Florida firebrands rushed to join the Jayhawkers in that territory. A virtual war was fought there for nearly two years while inflammatory speeches and editorials raised the emotional level on both sides.

A Free Black Man in a Slave Society

George Proctor was born free at St. Augustine during the second Spanish period and moved to Tallahassee with his father, Antonio Proctor, a Jamaican who had earned his freedom for services rendered to a Spanish governor. At Tallahassee, Proctor became a successful carpenter and built at least eight of the fine mansions that adorned the territorial capital. In 1839 he married a slave woman and purchased her freedom with $450 in cash and a note for $850. His wife was security for the mortgage. But a severe depression gripped Florida from the late 1830s until the mid-1840s and there was little construction going on. Proctor was unable to keep up payments on his note and Mrs. Proctor was repossessed. Proctor went to California, hoping to recoup his losses in the gold fields.

Mrs. Proctor's owner was Henry L. Rutgers, a prominent Tallahassee merchant. Her son, John Proctor, was born a slave, but he learned to read and write while working in Rutgers's store. During Reconstruction, he served as a state senator and later worked at Florida A&M College for many years. He died in 1937 when he was nearly one hundred years old.

In an interview in 1970, John's daughter explained that her grandfather had never returned from California, but she still owned a small pouch of gold dust that he had sent back in the 1850s and which the family had kept through good times and bad for more than 110 years. ➤

The demise of the Whig party left Richard Keith Call and his supporters in a quandary. They agreed with the Democrats about the necessity of protecting slavery but disagreed about the wisdom of leaving the Union. For the next few years, they attempted to forge a coalition of Florida Unionists under the banner of the Constitutional Union party. But they were unable to compete with the emotional Democrats. While the national party eked out a narrow victory for compromise candidate James Buchanan for president, the Florida Democrats elected Madison S. Perry, a strident member of the "South Carolina School" as governor. During the heated controversies of the late 1850s, Floridians heard the histrionics of their governor calling for secession from the Union.

When John Brown staged his raid on the U.S. arsenal at Harpers Ferry in 1859, he was hanged by Virginia authorities; his courage and sincerity led many to regard him as a martyr. Governor Perry seized the occasion to denounce "the John Brown villainy" and called for "eternal separation from the Union." Many Floridians agreed with the governor and came to equate the election of a Republican president with cause for secession.

A "Black Republican" President

Although the Constitutional Unionists made a valiant attempt to deter them, the Florida Democrats elected John Milton, a strong secessionist, as governor while the nation sent Abraham Lincoln, an Illinois Republican, to the White House.

The legislature finally agreed to appropriate funds for the militia, and Governor Perry began purchasing arms while "minutemen" were drilling all over the state amid intense excitement. In that context, an election was called for delegates to a convention to "consider the dangers incident to the position of the state in the Federal Union and to amend the constitution in any way necessary." When the convention assembled on January 3, 1861, its temporary chairman declared that Northern fanaticism had threatened Southern liberties and the election of "a wily abolitionist" as president left no hope for remaining in the Union. John C. McGehee, a staunch secessionist from Madison County, was elected chairman. George T. Ward, an old friend and political ally of Richard Keith Call, led a group of Unionists in efforts to delay action. On several ballots to delay, Ward and his followers lost by votes of about 30 to 39.

When it became clear that those favoring immediate secession had a majority, most of the Unionists joined them in a show of unanimity. Florida seceded from the Union on January 10, 1861, by a vote of 62 to 7. During an emotional ceremony on the east portico of the capitol, the consenting delegates signed the secession document while former Governor Call admonished them for their actions and predicted grim retribution to come.

Chapter 7

Civil War and
Reconstruction
1861–1877

WHERE THE BLOCKADERS CAME TOO LATE

Many of these soldiers pictured here were soon fighting miles away from where we see them now; a great many were drafted from New Orleans, from Mobile, Savannah, and Charleston; Florida and Georgia furnished their full quota to the Confederate army. This photograph was taken by Edwards, of New Orleans, who, like his confrère Lytle, succeeded in picturing many of the stirring scenes and opening tableaux of the war; they afterward took advantage of their art and used their cameras as batteries at the command of the Confederate secret service, photographing ships and troops and guns of the Federal forces, and sending them to the commanding generals of their departments. Over the chase of the gun is Pensacola harbor.

◄ *A young West Florida Seminary cadet. (Historical Association of South Florida)*

▲ *Elaborate sand batteries were constructed by the Confederates to protect against Union troops. However, many of these fortifications were poorly equipped and the cannon shot badly cast. (Pace Library—University of West Florida)*

◄ *A Florida camp in April 1861—possibly Cantonment Clinch located north of Bayou Chico in west Florida. Poorly supplied, many Confederate soldiers went without regulation uniforms. (Pace Library—University of West Florida)*

*W*hen Florida seceded from the Union in the spring of 1861, the Confederacy was already engaged in a shooting war with the nation many of Florida's citizens had worked so diligently to join only a few short years earlier. Finally obliged to decide where they stood, numerous Unionists joined their secessionist neighbors in support of their state. A minority, composed of some long-time Florida residents such as Richard Keith Call and newcomers from Northern states such as Calvin L. Robinson of Jacksonville, continued their loyalty to the United States, sometimes at considerable personal risk. Their Union beliefs eventually caused great difficulty for themselves and their Confederate antagonists, but their opposition was obscured in the early months of 1861 as one military unit after another marched away amid great excitement, well-wishing, and fanfare. Women sewed flags with militant slogans for their favorite units. Parades were held in honor of the departing soldiers, and the majority of the population acted as if the approaching war would be a mere outing. As months turned into years, lengthening casualty lists from the Virginia front dramatically altered that assumption.

Who Was in Charge?

Many institutional arrangements remained unchanged in secessionist Florida. A number of state and local officials retained their offices and continued to function as they always had. Charles H. Dupont, for example, was chief justice of the state supreme court in 1860, a position he retained throughout the Confederate period and into the postwar years. Many of the postmasters in Florida never resigned their positions but simply began sending their remittances to the Confederacy instead of the United States. The Confederate government was provisionally operational in a short time and assumed many of the functions formerly carried out by the United States at the same time it was taking over direction of the war.

In the meantime Florida acted as an independent, sovereign state. It raised a military force, acquired property from the United States, and equipped it with money appropriated by the state legislature. Partly because Florida was already dealing with the military situation while the Confederacy was being formed and partly because of the prevailing views regarding state sovereignty, the Florida government took the initiative in several areas that would subsequently cause conflicts with the Confederate government.

A Defenseless State

The most serious confrontation arose between the state and the new nation when Governor John Milton decided to defend Florida with the state's militia. With a population of about 140,000 — some 62,000 of whom were slaves — concentrated in the northern portion of the large state, and with about 1,200 miles of coastline to defend, the governor had a formidable task. Unfortunately for him, he was about to lose his armed forces. As the Confederacy gradually assimilated state militia units into a regular army, the central government decided that Florida's lengthy coastline and sparse population were not worth defending and soon ordered nearly all of the soldiers out of the state to fend off Union armies already advancing into the South.

Although dismayed at the abandonment of his state, Governor Milton tried valiantly to cooperate with the Confederate authorities while relying on a home guard for local defense. As a result, the long Florida coastline was left largely undefended throughout the war. Blockade runners plied the shallow waters with some success, although the Union blockading squadron was increasingly successful as the war progressed. There were numerous small engagements between amphibious Union forces and several independent cavalry units such as the one led by J. J. Dickison, and the Union occupied several sites along the coast at various times.

On the Periphery of the War

Although Florida sent a large proportion of its tiny population into the Confederate army and Floridians participated in all of the major battles from Shiloh in 1862 to the final bloody encounters in Virginia in 1864 and 1865, there were few major engagements in Florida itself. That did not, however, prevent the state from suffering considerable damage to its towns and property. Fernandina was occupied in early 1862 and remained in Union hands throughout the war. St. Augustine was occupied early in the war with the willing cooperation of some of its leaders, but Confederate forces were a constant threat to Unionists who wandered even a mile or two from the town. Both Pensacola and Apalachicola were occupied

▲ After Florida seceded from the Union in January 1861, the Confederate government ordered Lieutenant Slemmer to surrender Fort Pickens, located on Santa Rosa Island. Slemmer refused, and lame duck President James Buchanan negotiated a truce whereby Union forces would not bolster reinforcements if the Confederates would not attack. After Lincoln's inauguration, General Winfield Scott ordered the USS Brooklyn to reinforce the fort. Unaware of the trouble at Fort Sumter, Federal troops landed at Fort Pickens, breaking the truce. By April 16, 1861, the U.S. Navy ships Powhattan and Atlantic arrived with needed troops and supplies. This second reinforcement was depicted in Harper's Weekly. (Florida State Archives)

THE BATTLE OF SANTA ROSA, OCTOBER 9, 1861.—THE ATTACK UPON WILSON'S CAMP.—[SKETCHED BY MR. CHARLES F. ALLGOUER.]

▲ Harper's Weekly faithfully depicted scenes from the war, such as the attack on October 9, 1861, by Confederate troops on the Santa Rosa encampment of the Sixth Regiment of New York Volunteers, better known as Wilson's Zouaves. (Florida State Archives)

somewhat later, and while the Union took little interest in them, both were lost to the Confederacy.

A Whisper and a Wink

Key West remained in Union hands throughout the war. As the seat of the United States district court that adjudicated the disposition of all of the captured blockade-running vessels, the island community became a site for intrigue, spying, and extralegal exchanges of information as well as illegal exchanges of property. Many Confederate sympathizers stayed on the island, and some of them bid on the captured vessels that were sold at auction, purchased them, and sent them off to the Bahamas, from which place they were soon back in the blockade-running business.

Reduced to Ashes

Jacksonville was by far the most adversely affected Florida town during the Civil War. After the fall of Fernandina, Confederate forces withdrew from the teeming lumber port and a Union contingent stopped there on a reconnaissance mission along the St. Johns River. The Union soldiers were met by Calvin Robinson leading the Loyal Citizens of the United States, who had convinced General T. W. Sherman to help them establish a government loyal to the Union. Before that could be accomplished, however, Sherman was ordered out of the city, and Robinson and his associates, fearful of Confederate reprisal, departed with the Union army. During the ensuing years, they held meetings in New York and Washington and worked for a restored Union government in Florida, where they eventually gained some support.

In the meantime, there were confrontations along the lower reaches of the

An Unemployed Blockade Runner

When Spanish authorities captured the *Virginius* in 1873 and executed fifty-three of its crew members—several of whom were Americans—for smuggling guns to Cuban revolutionaries, an international incident was created. For a time attention focused on the controversial vessel, and then it was forgotten when the affair was resolved through diplomatic channels.

The ship already had a long and controversial history when it began running guns to Cuba. As the *Virginia*, it had first been a blockade runner for the Confederacy until the war ended in 1865. But slavery in the United States also ended at that time and the enterprising owner of the former blockade runner immediately saw opportunity in the change. Renaming his ship the *Virgin*, he ostensibly went into the lumber business. He hired crews of freedmen from Alabama and Florida to go "downcoast" to cut timber. Unfortunately for them, the next time the freedmen touched land was in Cuba, where slavery was still legal and there was a demand for their services. Having escaped bondage in the United States, they found themselves enslaved once again.

The situation came to light when Robert Toombs, who had gone to Cuba after the war to escape possible punishment for his Confederate activities, encountered his former carriage driver in Havana. The state department investigated the affair and discovered that several enterprising shipmasters were doing the same thing, but none were ever indicted.

▲ *A Confederate*
encampment at Pensa-
cola's Warrington Navy
Yard, 1861. (Pensacola
Historical Society)

St. Johns, and Jacksonville was again invaded in 1863. Led by Colonel Thomas Wentworth Higginson, a 1,400-member black troop raided Jacksonville, went up the river on a recruiting expedition that inspired a considerable number of slaves to join them, and eventually withdrew after destroying a significant portion of the town.

A Breadbasket for the Confederacy

By the time the black regiment left the St. Johns River, Floridians were feeling the severe effects of the war. Women no longer spent their time sewing colorful flags but were busy making shirts and underwear for their tattered soldiers in the field. With the help of a few disabled and older men and a slave force that remained remarkably loyal to them, the women raised hogs and grew great quantities of corn, much of which went to sustain Confederate armies in Virginia. But Florida's most important contribution to the food supply was beef. Jacob Summerlin, Francis A. Hendry, and other cattlemen who ran large herds on the open ranges of peninsular Florida drove thousands of cattle north for eventual consumption by Confederate soldiers. The drives were coordinated by Captain James McKay of Tampa.

By the latter part of 1863, the Florida cattlemen had competition from a Union force that occupied Ft. Myers and invaded the countryside in search of cattle for their own uses. The wharfs built by Union soldiers at Punta Rassa were subsequently used by Summerlin and other Florida cattlemen in the lucrative trade they established with Cuba after the war. The Union intrusion met considerable resistance from Florida's "Cow Cavalry."

A Military Expedition with a Political Flavor

The Union's interest in Florida's food supply coincided with Calvin Robinson's efforts to reestablish Union control in his adopted state. President Lincoln had dispatched John Hay, his private secretary, to Florida to help sign up Floridians willing to support a restored Union government. At the president's urging, General Truman Seymour was dispatched with troops to assist in the effort and to occupy northeastern Florida. Arriving in Jacksonville in early February 1864, Seymour was appalled at what he saw. The city was "a mere skeleton of its former self, a victim of war."

Whether the expanded Union occupation was intended to secure more potential voters for a restored government or to cut off the food being shipped from Florida to Virginia is not clear, but the general was shortly moving his army westward along the railroad toward Lake City. Confederate General Joseph Finegan was ordered to intercept his advance. On February 20, 1864, the two armies met at Ocean Pond near Lake City at the Battle of Olustee, the largest engagement in Florida during the Civil War. With approximately 6,000 troops on each side, the Confederates inflicted a severe defeat on the Union army, forcing it back to Jacksonville and Fernandina where it remained until the war ended.

The Battle of Natural Bridge

In early 1865, a combined operation by the Union navy and two Union cavalry regiments that had been recruited in Florida was launched to silence the gun

▲ *This Confederate camp, probably located at Big Bayou near Pensacola, is thought to be that of the Orleans Cadets Company A. (Pace Library—University of West Florida)*

batteries at St. Marks. Thwarted in their effort to cross the St. Marks River at Newport, the Union troops marched north to the natural bridge where the river ran underground. They were met there by Confederate troops and turned back. Although the Union force was headed for St. Marks, its defeat at the Battle of Natural Bridge has long been regarded by Floridians as a successful defense of their capital city. In fact, Tallahassee was the only Confederate capital east of the Mississippi not captured by the Union army.

The End of the War and the Beginning of Uncertainties

Satisfying as they were to the morale of a nearly despondent people, neither of the victories had any effect on the outcome of the war. Within weeks of the Battle of Natural Bridge, Lee surrendered in Virginia, and all organized Confederate resistance had been broken by May 1865. With their decimated population, disrupted economy, and uncertain political future, Floridians waited to see what price would be exacted from them by the victorious Union. They would have a while to wait. President Lincoln was assassinated within a week of Lee's surrender, and it was more than two months before Andrew Johnson, the new president, decided on a course of action. Even then his program was resisted by an increasingly hostile Congress, and Floridians were left wondering about their future.

Starting Over

In the meantime, soldiers straggled home to Florida singly or in small groups over a period of weeks. With a wagon and team borrowed from Union General John M. Schofield, General J. Patton Anderson returned to his Casabianca plantation in Jefferson County in a style similar to that to which he had been accustomed, but most of the soldiers walked back to their homes. They returned to a state quite different from the one they had left. Former slaves were free and

▲ *Requiring almost twenty years to complete, Key West's Fort Taylor became a Union stronghold during the Civil War. This painting is by General Seth Eastman. (Historical Association of Southern Florida)*

A Family Tragedy Averted by Shallow Water

There must have been few people for whom the Civil War was more tragic than Octavia Bryant Stephens, whose husband was shot and killed from ambush in 1864 after most of the war had been fought. But it might have been even worse.

When the Civil War began, Octavia and her husband, Winston Stephens, were living at Welaka, a community on the St. Johns that had been founded by her father, James W. Bryant. Octavia's husband joined a Confederate cavalry unit assigned to defend the St. Johns River region. Her father was out of the country when hostilities began, and the family was confounded when they learned that he had remained loyal to the Union.

Eager to visit his family even though that meant entering Confederate territory, Bryant obtained a pass and permission to ride up the river on a Union gunboat engaged in a military mission. When Confederate officials learned of the Union invader, Captain Winston Stephens was ordered to intercept it. Taking a position on Buffalo Bluff, Stephens and his unit lay in wait for the enemy vessel. As the boat came into view, it ran aground on a sandbar and was forced to turn back while still out of range. Captain Stephens was thus prevented from firing on an enemy vessel that he later learned was carrying his father-in-law. ◤

Union soldiers were in charge. It was planting time and something had to be done. Field commanders urged planters to establish a wage system by which life could continue. Over the next three years a new system of production emerged from that expedient measure. Some landowners continued to manage large acreages with the freedmen receiving a share of the crop as compensation. Others divided the land and rented it in small parcels to freedmen—and eventually to white tenants as well. The landlords' rights were protected by liens on the growing crops. The tenancy and crop lien system emerged as the primary method of farm production for several decades.

The Decline of Middle Florida

As railroads finally supplanted water routes to market, country merchants at the stations along the roads replaced the large port merchants of the ante-bellum period. Declining cotton prices over the next three decades and dismay over Reconstruction politics during the next ten years left the Middle Florida plantation belt in permanent decline. Apalachicola became a sleepy fishing port, experiencing only a minor revival when a firm began cutting and shipping cypress lumber there. Newport and St. Marks received only occasional visits by trading vessels. That was not the case with Jacksonville, which became the transportation hub of the state as interest shifted from the old plantation belt to the peninsula.

Between President and Congress and Fear of "Negro Rule"

President Andrew Johnson had inherited a growing controversy over the way the Union should be rebuilt after the war. Lincoln had wished a simple readmission of the seceded states to their former place in the Union. A congressional minority—the Radical Republicans—wanted to deny political rights to Southern leaders and to confer them on the freedmen. Johnson followed Lincoln's plan in the main but was finally thwarted by congressional opposition. Meanwhile, Florida remained under military occupation for about two years. When the Radical Republicans defeated Johnson and enfranchised blacks, many Floridians talked of migrating to Brazil, Mexico, California, and elsewhere rather than endure "Negro rule." Only a few actually left the state, but a sizable number of the inhabitants of Middle Florida boarded trains to Jacksonville from where they embarked on river boats to their new homes in the largely unsettled central Florida peninsula.

The Importance of One's Position

Although this may have been an exaggerated case, the departure of Mayor Francis Eppes from Tallahassee is indicative of the indignation Floridians felt toward the changes being imposed by the national government. During the struggle with the congressional Radicals, Andrew Johnson had proclaimed the restoration of civil law. Seizing the opportunity, Mayor Eppes arrested several soldiers for "fast riding" on the town's main street. General John Foster reminded the mayor that he had sole authority, and a heated exchange began. Foster ended the dispute with the terse comment: "Sir, you misapprehend the importance of your position." Eppes had had enough. Within weeks he was on his way to Orlando,

▲ *U.S. Congressman Josiah Thomas Walls, who represented Florida from 1871 to 1876. (Florida State Archives)*

▼ *A Jacksonville family out for a stroll probably in front of St. Paul's Methodist Church located at the northeast corner of Duval and Newnan streets. St. Paul's survived the Civil War and served its congregation until 1890, when it was sold to the Catholic church. The building was moved to a site across the street where it remained until a fire destroyed it in 1901. (Florida State Archives)*

◄ *Jonathan C. Gibbs became one of Florida's most distinguished black Reconstruction political leaders, serving as secretary of state from November 1868 to January 1873. He then became superintendent of public instruction until his death on August 14, 1874. (Florida State Archives)*

where he joined a growing number of immigrants from both Northern and Southern states.

River Boats, Yankee Promoters, and Citrus

In a day when railroads had not yet penetrated the peninsula, the region around Orlando enjoyed the advantages of an excellent water route via the St. Johns River. By the early 1870s, H. T. Baya, Frederick de Bary, and others were operating steamship lines on the river. The area received a boost when Henry S. Sanford announced plans to develop the 23,000 acres he had purchased on the south shore of Lake Monroe. With the aid of several hundred Swedish immigrants he brought to assist him, Sanford founded the town that bears his name, developed two orange groves—St. Gertrude's Place and Bel Air—publicized his sale of land to former President Ulysses S. Grant, helped start the South Florida Railroad to connect Orlando with the river steamers, and promoted the central Florida peninsula as a place where people of means could spend their winters in a balmy climate watching their planted orange groves grow.

Draining the Swamp

William Henry Gleason, after a stormy term as lieutenant governor of Florida and armed with a large grant of land, did much to publicize the attractions of the Florida peninsula. Starting at Miami but eventually settling at Eau Gallie, he demonstrated the feasibility of draining swampland and converting it to productive use. It was he who interested Hamilton Disston in the idea, and the Philadelphia saw manufacturer subsequently purchased four million acres of peninsular land with the idea of draining it and growing sugar cane.

Two Governors at Once

Although they were only in office for eight years during Reconstruction, the Florida Republicans provided current entertainment and future campaign material for the Democrats. One of the most bizarre episodes was the contest between Governor Harrison Reed and Lieutenant Governor William H. Gleason. The two had been elected in 1868 over the opposition of the radical faction of the party. When the defeated faction voted to impeach Governor Reed, they obtained the collusion of Gleason, as president of the senate, to adjourn the legislature without trying the governor. The furious Reed asked the state supreme court for an opinion as to whether he had been removed from office.

In the meantime, Reed continued as governor in the capitol building, while Gleason also claimed to be the chief executive with offices in the City Hotel across the street. The Democratic press was elated by the spectacle of two governors feuding for control of the state. They were further delighted when Adjutant General George B. Carse, a supporter of Reed who happened to be a U.S. Army captain on leave, caught Gleason trying to open the governor's safe and pistol-whipped him out of the building and down the street until the highly motivated pretender outran him.

The Supreme Court finally ended the comedy in December 1868 by ruling that Reed was still governor. As the rightful leader began removing from office all those who had supported Gleason, the *Savannah Republican* noted dryly that "Governor Reed is weeding his garden." ➤

▲ Cowboy Bone Mizell, whose exploits and folksy story-telling earned him the label "King of the Crackers." Artist Frederic Remington painted this portrait in DeSoto County in 1895. (University of South Florida Library— Special Collection)

▲ *Jacob Summerlin was a larger-than-life figure. Cattle baron, founder of cities, and philanthropist, he left his mark on the state. (Florida State Archives)*

▲ *Florida cowboys Archie L. Jackson (left) and Thomas McDonald (right). This photo was taken in the 1890s as the men were driving cattle from Old Town to Gainesville. (Florida State Archives)*

Cattle and the Open Range

The emergence of a citrus industry in peninsular Florida meant trouble for an already thriving enterprise, although it would be many years before the conflict became apparent. Since the 1850s a group of hardy individuals had capitalized on the existence of large numbers of cattle that had roamed Florida since the Spanish *conquistadores* brought the first specimens to the New World. Captain James McKay, Jacob Summerlin, Ziba King, John T. Lesley, Francis A. Hendry, and a few others had been herding huge droves of cattle on the open range since the 1850s. It was from these herds that cattle had been driven north for the Confederate army.

Florida Cattle and Cuban Gold

Long on cattle and short of cash, these drovers followed the lead of Captain McKay and began selling their stock in Cuba, where they were paid in Spanish gold. Often ranging over sixty miles, these drovers managed herds sometimes numbering 20,000 head. Each year they gathered the marketable animals and drove them to Tampa Bay, Punta Rassa, or other Gulf ports where they were loaded for shipment to Cuba. McKay's *Scottish Chief* was something of a flagship for the trade, but several other vessels engaged in the profitable business. Jacob Summerlin moved his headquarters from Bartow to Orlando in 1873 and, after settling a destructive range war that had beset the area, became one of the new community's founding fathers. James McKay continued as a prominent promoter of Tampa, which joined the peninsular boom in the early 1880s with the arrival of railroad transportation.

Beginnings of a Business Dynasty

In the meantime, one of McKay's daughters married Howell T. Lykes in 1874, and the basis was laid for one of the most important business empires in modern Florida. Not only would the Lykes Steamship Company transport many cattle to Cuba, but it would eventually engage in a worldwide shipping enterprise while other Lykes companies would process meat and citrus products for the domestic market.

An Early Tourist Attraction

Florida tourism gained considerably when H. L. Hart of Palatka, with a land grant from the state, cleared the snags from the Oklawaha River and made it navigable to Silver Springs. Using a specially designed steamer with a recessed paddle wheel, the Hart Line was carrying some 50,000 tourists annually to the beautiful spring by 1873. Palatka enjoyed some benefits as the St. Johns River site from which tourists embarked on their journey up the Oklawaha.

A New City in an Old Location

Jacksonville benefited enormously from the river activity. Having already gained favorable mention from Colonel John T. Sprague and other military commanders stationed in Jacksonville after the war, the city had rebuilt quickly as northern investors sought opportunity there. The St. James and other hotels were built to handle the growing number of winter tourists and prospective settlers. A new railroad depot and larger wharves emphasized the importance of the city as a transportation center. It was indicative of Jacksonville's growing importance as a financial center that William B. Barnett and his sons opened their bank there in early 1877.

An Uncertain Election and a Compromise Solution

As the economic focus shifted to the peninsula, where cattle, citrus, tourism, and lumber were much more important than cotton, the political center of the state remained in Middle Florida. It was there the Freedmen's Bureau took charge of the enfranchisement of the emancipated slaves and supervised labor relations between them and their former owners. The bureau was withdrawn in 1869, and although blacks continued to vote for a while and Republicans filled many offices, there was massive resistance from the white population. The matter came to a head during the fiercely contested presidential election of 1876.

Florida's determined Democratic party had nominated George F. Drew, a Madison County lumber operator, for governor and Noble A. Hull of Orange County for lieutenant governor. In a close contest they defeated incumbent Governor Marcellus L. Stearns and his lieutenant governor, David Montgomery, in the state race. But the results came only after almost four months of uncertainty about who the nation's president would be. After a bitterly fought campaign, Republican Rutherford B. Hayes defeated Democrat Samuel J. Tilden by an electoral college vote of 185 to 184. Although the state races had gone to the Democrats, Florida's electoral votes were counted for Hayes in a way that left considerable doubt as to the authenticity of his victory.

Although many Floridians doubted the Republican version of the electoral count, they accepted it in the belief that Hayes would bring an end to the more than ten years of national intervention in the internal affairs of the state. They turned out to be correct. No president used national troops to enforce civil rights in the South for nearly three-quarters of a century. The number of black voters declined rapidly, the Republican party was reduced to minority status, and the Democratic party—emphasizing white supremacy—took undisputed control of a Florida that was vastly different from the state that had joined the Confederacy in 1861. Drew's inauguration as governor—reinforced by repeated Democratic victories in subsequent elections—came to be called the "restoration of home rule" for Florida, and Drew was known as the "redeeming" governor. It would be many years before the question of the rights of the freedmen would be raised again.

▲ *In the late 1870s, Tallahassee's Adams Street retained a village charm. This view shows the old Union Bank Building (left) and the First Presbyterian Church (right). Located between the two buildings was "The Columns" mansion, a famous landmark which became the Dutch Kitchen Restaurant in 1949. (Florida Historical Society)*

Chapter 8

A State of the New
South: Northern
Investors, Railroads,
New Towns, and a
Cuban Expedition
1877–1900

◄ One of Florida's many railroad trestles, located at Lacoochee. Note the faint but recognizable group of men on the bridge in a handcar. (Florida State Archives)

▲ Frederick Leonard Tuttle and Julia DeForest Sturtevant pose for a wedding photo. Following the citrus freeze of 1895, Mrs. Tuttle sent Henry Flagler a snippet from one of her orange trees, suggesting that Flagler bring his railroad to the isolated hamlet of Miami, where winters were more moderate. (Historical Association of Southern Florida)

▲ *Handicapped by its wildernesses and swamps, Floridians relied on the state's many rivers as a means of inland transportation. Stern-wheelers such as the* Osceola *plied the waters during the golden age of steamboating. (University of South Florida Library—Special Collection)*

*T*he political struggles between Democrats and Republicans in the 1870s never interfered with bipartisan cooperation in economic matters. People of both political persuasions took advantage of a generous national policy according to which the state ultimately acquired nearly sixteen million acres of the public domain that was officially designated "swamp and overflowed land." While the classification was accurate in many areas, millions of acres of the best land in the state were also included. Intended to be used to encourage private investors willing to build transportation facilities to stimulate growth, the land had first to be extricated from a legal entanglement. In the 1850s Francis Vose had accepted bonds for supplies he sold to David Yulee's Florida Railroad. As guarantor of the bonds, the state had pledged its lands as security. Vose obtained a court injunction forbidding disposition of state land except for cash that was to be applied to his claim.

Reclaiming the State's Credit

Everyone realized the necessity of removing the injunctive cloud on the state's land. Both Republican administrations of the 1870s and their Democratic successors strove for a cash sale to satisfy the Vose heirs. They were unsuccessful until Hamilton Disston, visiting Florida at the invitation of his friend Henry Sanford, became interested in the drainage efforts of William Gleason and his Southern Inland and Navigation Company. Working with Democratic Governor William D.

Bloxham—sometimes referred to by friends and foes alike as "Slippery Bill"—Disston arranged with the Internal Improvement Fund trustees to buy four million acres of state land for $1 million in cash. The state was able to clear its land titles and at the same time acquire a new developer with means. Disston drained land, built railroads, began cultivating sugar cane, and built a handsome residence near St. Cloud. Although he died before finishing his projects, he brought extensive favorable publicity to the area between Orlando and the Pinellas peninsula and laid the basis for the modern sugar industry in southern Florida.

Plant and Flagler

Florida's reputation as a place where "invalids" might recoup their health combined with the availability of land to lure the two most famous of Florida's early developers. Henry Morrison Flagler and Henry Bradley Plant both saw Florida first when doctors told them their wives might improve their health there. Both men realized the possibilities of the warm climate and the vast reaches of undeveloped land.

Connecticut-born Plant came first in 1853 when his wife contracted tuberculosis. Having literally grown up in the railroad age, Plant found himself in Georgia when the Civil War began. Choosing to remain there and manage properties of several absentee Northern owners, he started the Southern Express Company after the War and made it a profitable enterprise while at the same time buying up several war-damaged railroads. He first entered Florida with an extension of his Savannah, Florida, and Western Railroad to St. Marks, but his completion of the Waycross Short Line in 1881 was the beginning of his interest in the peninsula. The Waycross Short Line gave Jacksonville its first direct rail service to northern destinations just at the time that city was becoming the entry point for

As Unfit for Them as They Are for It

In his 1875 travelogue on Florida, Sidney Lanier expressed disdain for the incarceration of more than seventy Indian prisoners from the west in the big fort at St. Augustine. "They are confined—by some ass who is in authority—in the lovely old Fort, as unfit for them as they are for it," he wrote. Among the last of the hapless people who were being rapidly removed from the westward path of white Americans in the late nineteenth century, the prisoners seem to have made the most of their incarceration.

Either to pass the time or to record their memories of their disappearing culture while they were still fresh—or both—the Indians displayed considerable artistic ability in drawing pictures depicting their life on the plains. Word of their presence at St. Augustine spread, and visitors came to view the "savages." They purchased the pictures and showed them to friends and relatives, and more visitors came to visit the fort. Soon the Indians were St. Augustine's most popular attraction, performing tribal dances, filling sketchbooks with their drawings, and receiving compensation for their efforts.

It was with mixed emotions that the people of St. Augustine looked on as the Indians departed. They had come to respect them for their abilities and to appreciate them for attracting visitors to the city, but most also agreed with Lanier who had written that he hoped "sincerely that they may all get out."

◀ Before Flagler's railroad came to Miami, many Biscayne Bay residents had only one source of cash income— starch making. Using the coontie root, a fern-like plant, thirty to forty pounds of starch could be produced by a single person and sold for three to five cents a pound on the Key West Market. (Historical Association of Southern Florida)

▶ Miami's business district in 1896. Known as Avenue D (now Miami Avenue), the street was unpaved and the businesses rough in appearance. This did not detract from the entrepreneurial spirit of early Miami businessmen, who willingly provided residents with the necessities of pioneer life, and some even offered the amenities of a more settled town. (Historical Association of Southern Florida)

◀ *Hamilton Disston's 1881 purchase of four million acres of Florida real estate opened up south Florida to development. Disston drained the Everglades, established agricultural colonies, and planted sugar on much of the reclaimed land, only to see his land empire crumble in the 1890s. (Tampa-Hillsborough Public Library)*

▶ *Palmetto Street in Ormond, Florida, in the 1880s. (Florida Historical Society)*

◄ *The small town of Luraville as it looked in the 1890s. A growing city on the Florida Railroad Line, the town boasted a thriving phosphate mining industry. A pump and watering trough standing in the center of the thoroughfare enabled town-goers to water their horses before embarking on their trip home. Note the frontier nature of the area, suggested by the man with the gun standing on the porch. (Florida State Archives)*

▼ *Employees of J. W. Carey's "Bargain Bazaar" display their merchandise in Key West. (Florida Historical Society)*

travel to peninsular Florida. Shortly after completion of the line to Jacksonville, Plant decided to extend his railroad to Tampa, then a tiny village that he called a "sand heap."

He next acquired the Jacksonville, Tampa, and Key West Railroad with tracks to Palatka and, in 1883, the South Orlando Railroad that operated from Sanford to Kissimmee. With the purchase of the charter of an unbuilt line from there to Tampa, he completed a rail line to Tampa in 1884. During the next ten years he acquired twenty-two short lines that were incorporated into the Plant system. By that time his railroad empire consisted of 1,665 miles of track, 600 miles of which were in Florida. A traveler could for the first time board a sleeping car at Tampa and ride to New York City without changing cars.

Henry Flagler first wintered in Jacksonville in 1878 with his ailing wife. After her death in 1881 and his remarriage, Flagler honeymooned in St. Augustine, which he decided to make his winter home. Construction of the fabulous Ponce de Leon Hotel began in 1885, and Flagler bought a small railroad that ran between Jacksonville and St. Augustine. When wealthy people shortly began following him to St. Augustine, Flagler conceived the idea that resulted in his Florida empire. With a fortune estimated at more than $50 million acquired through his partnership with John D. Rockefeller in the Standard Oil Trust, Flagler had the means to implement his ideas. Whether he built railroads to provide access to his hotels or constructed hotels so that passengers could ride his trains, it is clear that transportation and hotel facilities were intertwined in Flagler's grand scheme. By the time the Ponce de Leon was opened in 1888, he was already planning the Alcazar and the Cordova to cater to the less resplendent visitors to St. Augustine.

With the acquisition and rebuilding of several narrow-gauge lines, Flagler extended the services of his Jacksonville, St. Augustine, and Halifax River Railroad to Ormond Beach and Daytona by the late 1880s. With a land grant that promised about 8,000 acres per mile of railroad and offers of additional benefits from expectant landowners along his proposed route, Flagler sent his crews into the wilderness south of the Halifax River region in 1893. By the following year they were approaching Lake Worth, where West Palm Beach became railhead for a while. The Royal Poinciana was built to form the nucleus of Palm Beach. The Breakers and Flagler's Whitehall mansion were built soon after, and the exclusive settlement became the centerpiece of his Florida interests.

The Mother of Miami

Another believer in the future of south Florida was busily working for a railroad to her community by that time. Julia D. Tuttle, often called "the mother of Miami" and certainly its most avid proponent in the 1890s, had come to the Biscayne Bay area in 1875 from her home in Cleveland, Ohio, to visit her father, E. T. Sturtevant, a homesteader who was also a Republican state senator. After both her husband and father died, Mrs. Tuttle moved permanently to Florida in 1891. Recognizing the promise of the Biscayne Bay region and the necessity of adequate transportation to realize it, she first sought out James E. Ingraham, a personal acquaintance who had become president of Plant's railroad company. Although Ingraham was at first cool to the idea of extending a railroad from Tampa across the Everglades to the sparsely settled Miami community, he did

▲ *The* Fanny Knowles *offered excursion trips to guests at Henry Plant's posh Seminole* *Hotel in Winter Park in the 1880s. (Florida State Archives)*

▲ *Before Hawaii became easily accessible, Florida seemed the logical site for a U.S.-based pineapple indus-* *try. This lush pinery in Winter Haven bore such promise. The growth of Cuban pineapple plan- tations, along with* *insects and diseases, effectively stopped the industry in Florida. (Florida State Archives)*

lead an expedition across the sawgrass to investigate the possibility. But Plant rejected the idea.

By the time Plant decided against a Miami extension from Tampa, Flagler's railroad was being built toward Lake Worth and Mrs. Tuttle looked his way. The persistent woman received no encouragement from Flagler until nature intervened. When the freezes of 1894 and 1895 decimated the citrus region of central Florida, Mrs. Tuttle wrote Flagler that Miami had not been harmed. When Ingraham, who had then left Plant for Flagler's employ, affirmed her story, Flagler went to Miami to see for himself. Accepting the offer of Mrs. Tuttle and William B. Brickell to split their land with him, Flagler agreed to bring his railroad to Miami. A town was laid out, construction began on the Royal Palm Hotel, and a train entered Miami in early 1896 to the cheers of the entire population of about three hundred souls.

Completion of the Flagler System

By the time Flagler's Florida East Coast Railroad reached Miami, a substantial rivalry had developed between him and Plant. While the two exchanged occasional gibes, each extended his holdings. Flagler dredged Biscayne Bay and began operating the Peninsular and Occidental Steamship Line to Cuba and other Caribbean ports. By that time his road and his steamships were capable of carrying passengers to his string of hotels, which had a combined capacity for 40,000 guests. Flagler was also interested in carrying freight and encouraged the infant sugar industry around Lake Okeechobee by offering favorable rates. He also advocated production of pineapples and winter vegetables. Successful vegetable cultivation had to await better methods of dealing with the mucklands of the Everglades, but a flourishing pineapple industry existed along the Atlantic Coast for several decades.

Not content with his accomplishments, Flagler extended his railroad to Homestead in 1903 and took it to sea to reach Key West in 1912. He rode a train into the island city a few months before his death in 1913.

The Plant System and the Port of Tampa

While Flagler was building his line to Miami, Plant was busy extending his railroad southward to Port Tampa. The project was completed in 1887. With assistance from the U.S. government, a deeper channel was cut to open the port to large ocean-going ships, and by 1900 the port had the tenth largest customs receipts in the nation. Exports of cattle were also significant, along with growing quantities of citrus and phosphate. Pebble phosphate had been discovered in the Peace River in 1881. By the late 1890s, fifty-one companies were mining the rock. The new industry offered incentive to settle eastern Hillsborough County and the Peace River valley from Bartow to Charlotte Harbor. Much of the rock was shipped through Punta Gorda, but Port Tampa was the phosphate shipping center of the state.

The Plant Steamship Company extended southward to Key West and Havana and northward up the Apalachicola River to River Junction. Plant's hotel chain extended from the Seminole Hotel in Winter Park to several facilities along the

▲ *Payne's Prairie flooded in the 1800s when the drainage sink plugged up. This railroad trestle was built across Alachua Lake to carry produce to the hinterland. After the sink unplugged, the waters drained, leaving the prairie as it is today. James Calvert Smith of Tacoma, Florida, painted this watercolor as he remembered the lake in the 1890s. (Florida State Archives)*

◄ *In 1896, workmen began construction of Henry Plant's Belleview Biltmore, around which the city of Clearwater developed. (Tampa-Hillsborough Public Library)*

◄ *Company passes from Florida's golden railway age. (Historical Association of Southern Florida)*

▲ *Irish-born Charles W. Jones represented Florida in the U.S. Senate from 1875 to 1887. In 1884, he suffered a nervous breakdown attributed to overwork. Becoming irrationally infatuated with a wealthy lady form Detroit, he neglected his duties, following her to Detroit. His erratic behavior and his absenteeism from the Senate became headline news that ended his political career. He was widely caricatured as Florida's "love-mad" senator. (Florida Historical Society)*

The Flagler Divorce Law

Henry Flagler was unfortunate in marriage. After his first wife died in the early 1880s, he married her nurse and they lived happily for several years before she began losing her mind. According to one story, she calmly announced at breakfast one morning that she was planning to marry the czar of Russia. Whether or not the story is accurate, it soon became clear that she was hopelessly insane. Flagler apparently did not wish to remain shackled to the unfortunate woman, but there was no legal way he could end the marriage at the time.

There were many rumors about the reasons for its majority approval when a law passed the 1901 legislature providing for divorces in cases strikingly similar to Flagler's. Apparently the only person ever to take advantage of the law, he was divorced shortly after the measure was enacted. It was repealed by the 1905 legislature. There is little wonder that the measure is still referred to as the Flagler Divorce Law. ➤

Gulf. The crown jewel of his hotel enterprise was the eclectically styled Tampa Bay Hotel (now the University of Tampa), which has been a landmark on the Hillsborough River since its grand opening celebration in early 1891. Plant died in 1899, too soon to know of Flagler's overseas extension to Key West. His railroads were reorganized in 1901 as the Atlantic Coast Line, while Flagler's still operates—with many changes and after a decades-long battle for control—as the Florida East Coast Railroad.

More Railroads

The Seaboard Airline Railroad took over several older railways in Florida and reached Tampa in 1886. At about the same time, the Southern Railroad extended its lines through the central peninsula toward Charlotte Harbor. The other major line that served Florida in the age of railroad travel was the Louisville and Nashville. Under the leadership of William Dudley Chipley, a fervent promoter of Pensacola, the Florida division of that line linked western Florida to the rest of the state at River Junction in 1883. It also opened rail service from the Midwest to the Florida peninsula just as the region was beginning to boom in the 1880s.

Railroads, Cigars, and the Rise of Tampa

The arrival of Plant's railroad in 1883 awakened Tampans to the entrepreneurial spirit of the New South, and a board of trade was soon looking for ways to stimulate growth. It was a fortunate blending of interests when Vicente Martínez Ybor, Ignacio Haya, and Gavinox Gutierrez visited Tampa Bay in search of suitable sites for cigar factories. Having moved from Cuba to Key West during the first Cuban revolution (1868–1878), they sought a better situation than the island city offered. Finding in Tampa a suitable climate, an excellent transportation system, and a receptive board of trade, they struck a bargain. With a grant of land and the good offices of the board of trade, Ybor laid out the city that bears his name in 1885. By the following year cigars were being manufactured even as the Ybor Land and Development Company strove to induce other producers to move there. He and Haya were soon joined by Eduardo Manrara, Emilio Pons, and many others.

◄ *The forerunner of the National Guard, state militias served as protectors of their particular region. From Pensacola, the Fourteenth Company of Florida Guards, a black regiment, drills in crisp formation in the 1890s. (Pensacola Historical Society)*

▲ *Yellow fever, also known as broken bone fever and yellow jack, was the scourge of nineteenth-century Florida. In this scene refugees of the epidemic are turned back. (Florida State Archives)*

▲ *The Dozier House, across from the Episcopal church in Cedar Key, is indicative of the lifestyle of that town's affluent residents in the 1890s. Many Florida homes feature windmills that served as water pumps. (Florida State Archives)*

▼ This once-productive orange grove near Caldwell lay desolate after the freeze of 1886. Although new growth is evident on some of the trees, it would take years before the grove returned to its prefreeze production rate, only to be hit again by the devastating freezes of 1894 and 1895. (Florida State Archives)

Although the Cuban workers at first found the location inhospitable, Ybor induced his employees to stay and they eventually formed a viable community. They were joined by Italians, many of whom had come to Florida to work in the sugar cane fields and on the railroads, and by Spaniards who had long been engaged in cigar manufacturing in their native land. With their differing cultural backgrounds, these new immigrants sometimes clashed, but they gradually developed a distinctive community. Although the Latin community of Ybor City and its counterpart, West Tampa, long remained largely separated from Tampa's Anglo society, the Latins eventually merged with the other Tampa to give that city a distinctively diverse culture.

The manufacture of fine, hand-rolled cigars at Tampa stimulated the production of shade-grown tobacco in Gadsden County where it remained a major crop for many years. Factories were opened in other Florida cities, but Tampa dominated the industry. By 1900 there were more than one hundred cigar factories there producing one hundred million cigars each year.

The Great Freezes of 1894–1895

The open-range cattle industry remained important throughout the peninsula from Brooksville where the Lykes family was headquartered to Brevard County on the Atlantic Ocean and southward to the Everglades, but citrus was becoming the glamour crop of peninsular Florida. Harriet Beecher Stowe's grove on the St. Johns River near Mandarin exemplified those of many winter residents who planted groves and left them to be tended by others during the summer months. But permanent residents also planted groves, and by the early 1890s a considerable citrus crop was being produced. Growers were still searching for suitable marketing methods and reliable transportation facilities when they were suddenly confronted with a more immediate problem.

The lobby of the San Juan Hotel in Orlando had become an unofficial citrus exchange where growers and buyers gathered and negotiated the sale of crops on the trees. A crowd was there on Christmas Day, 1894, and intense bidding was being coolly received by growers hoping for better prices. When the temperature began dropping in the early afternoon, growers became more receptive as buyers began withdrawing their offers. By late evening the temperature had dropped about sixty degrees and remained below freezing for several days. The fruit and some new growth were destroyed, but most growers resolved to wait for next year. The weather warmed over the next several weeks and the trees put out new growth. Then, on February 7, 1895, the temperature plunged below 20 degrees. The sap-filled trees literally exploded and the majority of them were killed to the ground. The citrus industry was destroyed by the back-to-back freezes. Where five million boxes of fruit had been grown in 1893–94, fewer than one million boxes were produced two years after the freezes. The citrus industry eventually recovered and exceeded all expectations, but not until well into the twentieth century.

Harvesting the Forests

Another burgeoning industry provided employment for some central Floridians

▲ In June 1898, Cocoa residents held a fish fry in honor of the Second Regiment of Louisiana Volunteers, who would soon be leaving for the war front in Cuba. (Florida State Archives)

▲ A 350-pound green turtle is lifted from a kraal located in Key West in April 1885. A delicacy for gourmets, such turtles were frequently shipped north to New York stockpots. (Florida State Archives)

▲ Punta Rassa gained fame first as a shipping point for Florida longhorns destined for Cuba. Then, in the 1860s, the Inter-Ocean Telegraph Company laid a telegraph cable along the community's Gulf waters. In 1898, Punta Rassa received the first cable transmit- tals of the sinking of the USS Maine and relayed the message to the rest of the country. (Florida State Archives)

◄ This camp in Miami, photographed in 1898, resembled others that sprang up near exit ports for men preparing to embark on the ships that would take them to the battle front of the Spanish-American War. Whole families joined those men waiting to go to the war zone. (Historical Association of Southern Florida)

while they waited for the groves to become productive again. With over half of its land covered by virgin longleaf pine and additional expanses of cypress and hardwoods, Florida had long been recognized as an excellent site for lumbering. But it was not until the latter decades of the nineteenth century that the production of yellow pine lumber and the associated manufacture of turpentine and gum resin became major Florida industries.

Many of the short railroads that had been absorbed by the Plant, Flagler, and other trunk lines had begun as logging roads. As the trunk lines were completed and harbors were improved at Jacksonville, Tampa, and Pensacola, lumber and naval stores became major exports from all of them. Logging camps and turpentine farms were scattered throughout the forests, gradually moving southward from the Georgia line as older stands of timber were cut out. Huge stacks of freshly sawn lumber, crossties, and poles suitable for ship masts stood alongside thousands of barrels of turpentine and gum resin in the rail yards and on the docks during the half century between the Civil War and World War I—and in diminishing quantities for several decades thereafter.

The Second Cuban Revolution

Concern about the disaster in the citrus belt was soon overshadowed by news coming out of Cuba. Perhaps because of the recency of the Civil War and the disruption of Reconstruction, Americans had shown little interest in the Cuban struggle for independence between 1868 and 1878, but they were much more attentive to renewed strife in the 1890s. Whether out of concern for the growing number of his Cuban-born constituents or a genuine belief in the right of self-determination, Senator Wilkinson Call had filled the pages of the *Congressional Record* as well as his speeches back home with references to *Cuba Libre* for years before the outbreak of hostilities. Americans in general and Floridians in particu-

▲ The apostle of Cuban liberty, José Martí made several trips to Florida determined to raise public and financial support for Cuba Libre. During one such trip to Key West, Martí visited Teodoro Peréz, a factory owner and secretary of the Cigar Manufacturers Union. Standing behind the little girl on the upstairs balcony, Martí is shown with a group of supporters at Peréz's home located at Duval and Catherine streets. The building now operates as La Terraza de Martí's guest house and restaurant. (Historical Association of Southern Florida)

lar were further aroused by the strident voices coming from well-organized Cuban patriotic groups in Tampa. The readers who were employed to entertain the cigar rollers in the factories helped infuse zeal for the forthcoming revolution.

Arriving at Tampa in late 1891, the revolutionary leader José Martí was welcomed by cheering crowds and the open pockets of generous supporters. Nearly all the Cubans in the cigar factories contributed a day's salary for the cause. The Cuban Revolutionary party kept the movement alive from its inception in 1892 and Martí returned for several visits. Plans for the revolution were hammered out in Tampa and the signal for the beginning of hostilities came from there. Wrapped inside a Havana cigar, the message was delivered to revolutionary groups in Cuba that February 24, 1895, was the day. News of hostilities was received by wild cheering in Tampa, with interest by most Americans, and by a determination to act on the part of several spirited adventurers.

The Filibustering Sheriff

Among those was Napoleon Bonaparte Broward, an experienced river pilot who had gained extensive publicity as the strong-willed sheriff of Duval County and who was destined to even greater notoriety for his efforts to supply arms to the Cubans in defiance of U.S. neutrality laws. With his brother and a friend, Broward sailed his tug, the *Three Friends*, into Cuban waters, where he was captured by the U.S. Coast Guard. When war broke out between the United States and Spain in 1898, Broward, like several other captains who had participated in more than one hundred gun-running missions to the island, was under indictment for his actions. The charges were eventually dropped, and instead of becoming a convict, Broward soon became governor of Florida.

Remembering the *Maine*

While quite willing to provide moral and physical support to the Cuban revolutionaries, many Floridians were unenthusiastic about U.S. intervention. Some were concerned that the coastal cities might be subjected to Spanish attack, while

▼ *An 1880 illustration of Harriet Beecher Stowe's home, situated on the banks of the St. Johns River near Mandarin. (Florida Historical Society)*

Harriet Beecher Stowe in Florida

After the Civil War, Harriet Beecher Stowe became a winter resident of Florida and a tourist attraction as well. She and her husband purchased a house and an orange grove at Mandarin on the St. Johns River just above Jacksonville. As more and more people traveled upriver, one enterprising steamer captain saw an opportunity at the Stowe residence.

He arranged with Mrs. Stowe to listen for a certain series of blasts from his boat whistle. That was the signal for the famous author to come out on her porch and sit at a desk, pen in hand. The captain would then explain that the vessel was approaching the winter home of Harriet Beecher Stowe and that, if they were fortunate, they might be able to see the author busily at work on her next novel. During the winter months, they were usually fortunate. After the steamer passed out of sight, Mrs. Stowe was free to go back to whatever she had been doing before the interruption. It was only a small fabrication, however, since she did write a novel while in Florida during the post–Civil War years.

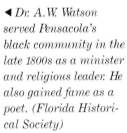

◄ Mrs. Adams, known as Aunt Memory, was born in slavery. She was brought to Tallahassee at the age of twenty-four and sold to a Mr. Argyle for $800. An enterprising woman, Aunt Memory traveled to the 1893 Chicago World's Fair, where she sold enough photos of herself to finance her trip. (Florida State Archives)

◄ Dr. A.W. Watson served Pensacola's black community in the late 1800s as a minister and religious leader. He also gained fame as a poet. (Florida Historical Society)

▼ In 1895, these members of the Pensacola Colored Women's Auxiliary Board represented their club at the Atlanta Exposition, where Booker T. Washington made his famous speech. Auxiliary boards were often responsible for running hospitals, nursing homes, orphanages, and other charitable organizations. (Florida Historical Society)

▼ A freedman plows a furrow near his Middle Florida homestead in the 1890s. A gaunt ox assists in the arduous task. (Florida State Archives)

▲ *Fort Matanzas near St. Augustine was built in 1742 to protect the city from enemy attack by way of the inland waterway. The fort, shown here as it appeared in 1885, fell into neglect during the second Spanish period, receiving needed face-lifts in 1916 and 1920. The name Matanzas, Spanish for "slaughter," commemorates the spot where Menéndez massacred French Huguenots. (Florida Historical Society)*

▲ *Spanish prisoners, captured in Cuba, pose at Key West before transport to Miami. (Historical Association of Southern Florida)*

others feared that Cuba might be annexed to the United States and replace Florida as the destination for winter tourists. But tension mounted as newspapers reported sensational stories of Spanish mistreatment of the Cubans. Many Americans seemed anxious for military action. An ambivalent President McKinley worked with the Spaniards for a diplomatic solution while sending the USS *Maine* to Cuba in a show of strength. When the vessel was blown up by still unknown parties, the president gave in to public demand and called for war. Congress complied and the nation prepared for armed hostilities in the summer of 1898.

Preparation for War

All of Florida's coastal communities demanded defense installations, and most of them lobbied to become the staging center for an assault on Cuba. Flagler and Plant each recognized an opportunity to use their transportation facilities and to promote their cities. While 7,000 soldiers were sent to Miami where they spent two months raising havoc with the local citizenry, Tampa was designated to receive the Cuban expeditionary force. More than 30,000 troops were stationed at Camp Cuba Libre near Jacksonville, and others spent a few weeks at Fernandina and Lakeland.

While all the communities received national attention, the action was at Tampa. With its population suddenly more than doubled to about 66,000, the city's accommodations were far outstripped by demand. Closed for the season, the Tampa Bay Hotel was reopened to house military officers and the newspapermen and was reportedly filled to capacity for the first time since it opened in 1891. The hotel received favorable notice, but the surrounding community was decried as an uncomfortable sand heap. While enjoying the volume of traffic on his railroad and steamships, Plant recognized that the war would be a short one and declined to expand his facilities to accommodate a temporary demand. A single track carried the load between the city and Port Tampa. Supply-laden freight cars preceded their invoices and confounded supply personnel, while the post office and the telegraph office were overwhelmed by the volume of communications. Worst of all was the problem of entertaining thousands of soldiers while they waited for embarkation. Some of the regiments were assigned to Port Tampa and Lakeland, but the vast majority remained at Tampa where they complained of heat, sand, boredom, and "embalmed beef," a contaminated ration that ultimately scandalized the nation.

Despite inadequate housing and transportation, rampant confusion, and occasional disorder, Tampa businessmen and less reputable entrepreneurs were delighted. The first payroll in May exceeded a quarter of a million dollars and approached one million dollars before the troops embarked. Merchandise was swept from shelves while dance halls, gambling casinos, and sporting houses scarcely kept up with demand.

The Invasion of Cuba

General William R. Shafter, probably the fattest man ever to lead men in battle, finally received orders to embark for Cuba, but not before his force was joined by the Rough Riders, commanded by Colonel Leonard Wood and volubly

36 LIVE ALIGATOR AND CRACKER TEAM, ORLANDO, FLA.

◄ With Florida's numerous groves of scrubby pines and the availability of cheap labor, turpentine stills and naval stores became one of the state's most profitable and important sources of income. This is Agnew's Still on Silver Spring Run in the 1880s. (Florida State Archives)

▲ Alligator wrestling enlivens an Orlando afternoon in the 1880s. (Florida State Archives)

assisted by Lieutenant Colonel Theodore Roosevelt. During its stay of less than a week, the Rough Rider regiment won the hearty approval of Tampans, while its second-in-command bedazzled them even more. On June 14, 1898, thirty-five ships carried about 16,000 troops and their supplies to Cuba. After a desultory show of resistance and the destruction of Admiral Cervera's naval force, the Spanish government sued for peace, and the U.S. Army personnel, now beginning to suffer from tropical diseases, was reassigned to the cooler climes of Long Island. Theodore Roosevelt, who capitalized enormously on the publicity he received during the summer war, later lamented that "it wasn't much of a war, but it was the only one we had."

Begun in the early summer and ended before autumn, the Spanish-American War was followed by Cuban independence from Spain and a lengthy U.S. occupation, but American officials kept their promise not to annex the island. Nevertheless, lying only ninety miles from Florida, Cuba was continually influenced by its giant neighbor, and the relationship between Cuba and Florida was a continuing one.

Into the Twentieth Century

Florida had received some unfavorable publicity from the diseases and other tribulations afflicting the soldiers in some of the camps, but the overall effect of

▲ While freed from the slavery-imposed role of "mammy," black women were still highly valued as nursemaids of white children. A black nurse with her young charge in St. Augustine in the 1890s. (St. Augustine Historical Society)

the war was beneficial. The economic stimuli to the communities where soldiers were stationed infused money into the economy that had so recently been devastated by the citrus freeze. Both the Plant and Flagler systems had benefited from the increase in traffic, and both Miami and Tampa were called to the attention of the nation. Despite the criticism, the overall affect of the exposure was an acceleration of the state's growth in the early twentieth century. Some wondered what the effect might have been had the little war occurred during the winter months.

While the Spanish-American War tended to bind the sectional wounds of the nation that had lingered since the Civil War, it had diverted the attention of Floridians from issues challenging the existing political arrangements in the state. The older Democratic leaders who had regained control of the state from the Republicans in the 1870s were passing from the scene. They were about to be replaced by a new generation that carried into the twentieth century some of the old but also much that was new.

▲ *Draped with the gingerbread stamp of the 1880s, the DeFuniak Springs Library in Walton County was founded and built by the Ladies Library Association. Although additions have since been made, the original library is still being used. (Pace Library—University of West Florida)*

◀ Teaching represented one of the very few occupations acceptable for women of the middle and upper classes in the nineteenth century. Mrs. Frances Wright of Lakeland, widowed in the 1870s, chose to support herself and her young daughter by teaching painting. Mrs. Wright poses with her class, c. 1888. (Florida State Archives)

◀ Residents of Alachua County gather at Oak Hall Park in Gainesville to root for their local team in the 1890s. Floridians like to believe that baseball first gripped Abner Doubleday while the soldier campaigned in the Everglades in 1857. (Florida State Archives)

▶ A Volusia County hunting party in the 1890s, made up mostly of women, dispels the myth that hunting was solely a man's sport. (Florida State Archives)

Chapter 9

Progressive Politics,
Peninsular Growth,
and World War
1900–1919

◀ This awkward-look-
ing machine was used
to clear land along the
Gulf Coast in 1919,
probably in preparation

for a new development
or large farm. (Tampa-
Hillsborough County
Public Library)

▲ Recognized as one of
Miami Beach's most
important developers,
Carl F. Fisher relaxes
in the sun on his island
paradise. (Historical
Association of Southern
Florida)

▲ *Two elderly St. Augustine residents enjoy the excitement of a sightseeing cruise over the city. While the pilot looks fairly competent, his passenger appears to be slightly apprehensive. An interesting question concerns the location of the photographer. (St. Augustine Historical Society)*

*T*he early years of the twentieth century were busy ones in Florida and throughout the nation. From the local communities, through the state houses, and all the way to Washington, a spirit of enthusiasm and optimism, faith in the future, and a desire to improve were rampant. With one technological achievement after another—the telephone, electric power, the automobile, the airplane—Americans saw ways of making their lives better. At the same time, most recognized that the application of these inventions to their daily lives would mean a greater reliance on collective action. They looked to their governments—local, state, and national—for assistance. Two direct results of such beliefs were the expanding role of government at all levels and the increased interdependence of individuals. Inspiration was added when Theodore Roosevelt, catapulted into the presidency by his self-promotion and an assassin's bullet, began using his new office, which he regarded as a "bully pulpit," to advocate "progressive" policies.

The Broward Era

While Florida continued to rely on wealthy individuals to spearhead growth, the state acquired a dynamic leader of its own in Napoleon Bonaparte Broward who, like Roosevelt, had benefited greatly from the publicity resulting from his role in the Cuban independence movement. Broward and his reform-minded associates advocated broad expansion of government services while also urging continued growth and development. During the terms of Broward, Albert W. Gilchrist, and Park Trammell (from 1905 to 1917), the state established a university system; extended assistance to a strengthened public school system; gave the railroad commission effective regulatory authority; made the electoral system more democratic through the direct primary; implemented a prison system; began conservation of fish, wildlife, and forests; and established the state road department.

Water Runs Downhill

Governing a population of slightly more than 500,000, Broward still understood progress to mean development of the state's vast expanse of unused land, and he exerted his greatest energies in efforts to drain the Everglades. Observing that "water runs downhill," Broward thought that drainage would be a simple matter of opening a few canals and allowing the surplus water to run into the ocean. What seemed to be a situation of too much water eventually proved to be infinitely more complex, and after more than half a century of cooperation between the national government, the state, and various combinations of private developers, it is now generally understood that tampering with the Everglades was not a good idea in the first place. But hindsight notwithstanding, it was a progressive idea in 1905 to drain the wetlands and open them to cultivation. After the expenditure of large sums and the eventual recognition that water control in both wet and dry times was essential, the land was opened to cultivation, and great quantities of sugar cane, vegetables, and cattle have since been raised in the wetlands. It was well into the 1920s, however, before that productivity was achieved. In the meantime, more and more people turned to Florida as a place to invest, to visit, and to live.

▼ *A sugar cane mill in Hillsborough County. The horses were used to grind the cane, which was then boiled down into syrup or " 'lasses." (Tampa-Hillsborough County Public Library)*

▲ *Mrs. Minnie Gaskin and her class at Pensacola's No. 3 Elementary School about 1900. (Pensacola Historical Society)*

▼ *The class of the Alva Consolidated School, on the Caloosahatchee River around 1900. Note that all of the boys are barefoot while all* *the girls are wearing shoes. (Fort Myers Historical Society)*

Creation of Miami Beach

While the governor was campaigning for his large-scale drainage program, individuals were proceeding with their own plans for reclaiming wetlands. Miami was still the base from which construction was proceeding on Flagler's overseas railroad to Key West when John Collins and Carl Fisher met. Collins had lived at Miami nearly a quarter of a century when he began his efforts to grow avocados on a spit of sand known as Ocean Beach. He soon turned his project into a real estate venture, but by 1913 he and his partners had run out of funds. On a visit to Miami, Carl Fisher of Indianapolis, who had made a fortune in the budding new automobile industry, became interested in Collins's faltering project and revitalized it with an infusion of a half-million dollars. They employed Edward E. "Doc" Dammers, an auctioneer whose sales had become major entertainment features from Palm Beach to Miami, to auction land even as a bridge was still being completed. Fisher employed a large crew of workmen who scooped up millions of cubic feet of sand from Biscayne Bay and covered what had been a mangrove swamp to make Miami Beach.

The Dixie Highway

The creation of Miami Beach was only the first of Fisher's ambitious projects. In the heyday of the steam locomotive, Flagler had built a railroad to the tip of the nation's southernmost state. Fisher belonged to the coming age of the automobile, and his dream was to build a highway connecting Miami with Chicago. Not only did he succeed, but his efforts affected the entire state of Florida.

When it was learned that Fisher's Dixie Highway Association was planning an automobile road through the state to Miami, many communities formed their own associations to ensure that their town was on that road. There was dismay in the central Florida ridge district when the Dixie Highway Association met at Chattanooga, Tennessee, and selected a circuitous route through Tallahassee to Jacksonville and down the coast. Frenzied lobbying resulted in a compromise according to which there would be an eastern and a western route. The original coastal route was supplemented by another that wound through Gainesville, Ocala, Orlando, Kissimmee, Bartow, and Arcadia, rejoining the other road at Palm Beach. While both routes defied the maxim about the shortest distance between two points, they satisfied a large number of local boards of trade throughout the state.

In 1915, Fisher led an automobile cavalcade from the Midwest to Miami, reaching that city in October where about one thousand Miamians met him in a joyous celebration. Everyone predicted a flow of people and new money into the state as a result of Fisher's achievement. They could scarcely have anticipated the extent of the accuracy of that prediction.

A Causeway across the Everglades

Automobile fever was an epidemic by 1915. While Fisher was pushing his Dixie Highway, James F. Jaudon called for a road to connect Miami with Tampa. Work began on the Tamiami Trail under the auspices of Dade County in 1915, but that was only a beginning. With the cooperation of Barron Collier and the state road department—and the use of millions of sticks of dynamite—a limestone causeway

▲ *Rural roads in Florida were rough and constantly in danger of flooding from swamps and heavy rains. (Florida State Archives)*

◀ *Dredging canals was one of the first steps in the construction of the Tamiami Trail, which began in 1915. (Florida State Archives)*

▼ *In 1922, crews prepare for the construction of the Gandy Bridge. This 2.5-mile bridge connected St. Petersburg and Tampa, cutting travel distance from 43 to 19 miles. The brainchild of George Gandy, the structure was proclaimed the world's longest auto toll bridge. (Florida Historical Society)*

was built above the muck, and the road was opened in 1928 during the administration of Governor John W. Martin.

The Gandy Bridge

A phenomenon of the 1920s just like the Tamiami Trail, the Gandy Bridge across Tampa Bay was also conceived in 1915. Tampa had spread out along the eastern shore of the bay by the early 1900s. Across the bay St. Petersburg, little more than a railroad station at the end of Peter Demens's Orange Belt Railroad in the late 1880s, had also grown into a sizable winter resort. Walter Fuller was enjoying a land boom there as he undertook an extension of Central Avenue to the Gulf. As the number of automobiles increased in the bay area, drivers were impressed by George Gandy's idea of shortening the nearly fifty-mile drive between the two cities with a bridge across the bay. Although it was not completed until 1924, the bridge cut the mileage between Tampa and St. Petersburg by more than half.

Without a Dollar in His Pocket

H. Carl Dann, who touted himself as the man who "was born without a dollar in his pocket," is representative of the homegrown variety of Florida developer. Born in Orlando, Dann developed sixty-one different projects in and around his home town between 1910 and the late 1920s. He was successful in building suburban housing, country clubs, and hotels, but his most ambitious project was a grand failure.

Borrowing from the ideas of both Governor Broward and Carl Fisher, Dann decided to develop the area north of Lake Apopka, the largest concentration of muckland in the state outside the Everglades. To develop the "super garden spot of the Universe," Dann organized a company with branches in several northern cities, contracted for transportation with the Deluxe Bus Lines of Orlando, and began tours of the Zellwood area for potential buyers. His idea was to grow potatoes, which were in short supply as World War I began. A number of lots were sold and "a giant crop of spuds" was planted. But the muckland was too much for them. The potatoes grew but rotted as soon as they were gathered. The Zellwood mucklands were not productive until the 1940s, after much had been learned about muck farming in the Everglades. Dann's promotion of the area, like that of others along the routes of the Dixie Highway, brought many visitors to the state and helped prepare the way for the boom of the 1920s.

The Birthplace of Speed

In the 1890s, Floridians caught the bicycle craze that was sweeping the nation. Bicycle paths were built around and between many communities, and Sunday afternoons were often spent on the paths. Bicycle mania led indirectly to the Daytona Beach Speedway. Vacationing at the Ormond Hotel in 1902, James Hatheway noticed that bicycle tires left little imprint on the ocean beach. Reasoning that the impacted sand would also be a good surface for automobiles, he began promoting an auto race there. Within a few months, Barney Oldfield, Alexander Winston, William K. Vanderbilt, and other enthusiasts were racing their cars on

◀ *Taking a break from a country outing, these bicyclists rest by the side of a north Florida road, c. 1880s. (Florida State Archives)*

▼ *Drivers line up before a race on Ormond Beach. (Florida State Archives)*

▶ *Windsailing on the beach at Ormond in 1903, a popular sport of Floridians and tourists. The pedal-propelled chairs in the background were known as "Afromobiles" because the chairs were usually driven by black drivers. (Florida State Archives)*

▲ *Employees at the O. L. Stephens sawmill in Concord, Florida. (Florida State Archives)*

the beach at speeds as high as 57 miles per hour. The idea caught on quickly. Henry Flagler built the Ormond Garage, which housed one hundred cars. The Florida East Coast Automobile Association was formed, and races were soon attracting drivers from all over the world. When races were about to begin, fire bells clanged and stores, offices, and schools closed so that thousands could attend.

Beach racing continued intermittently until after World War II, by which time automobiles had become so powerful that beach racing was simply too dangerous. During the 1950s, Bill France built the Daytona International Speedway, and the first Daytona 500 was held in 1959. Since that time, a full racing agenda has been added, and the "World's Most Famous Beach" has been left to pleasure seekers.

Florida Panhandle and Alabama's Coast

An accident of timing had made the area west of the Apalachicola and south of the 31st parallel a part of Florida. Choosing to become a state in 1819 rather than await the transfer of Florida from Spain in 1821, Alabama sought repeatedly to acquire what was viewed as her natural seacoast. When the last attempt in 1901 failed, it seemed clear that Pensacola was destined to remain Florida's western-most city. Connected to the rest of the state by the Louisville and Nashville Railroad after 1883, Pensacola had developed as a lumber and naval stores shipping port and as the trading center for a sizable area of west Florida and southern Alabama. The vast forests were being cut out by the beginning of World War I, however, and a surge in the volume of cotton shipments did not affect the decline.

◄ *This attractive waterfront structure, located on Miami Beach, was the home of T. S. Pancoast. The trappings of an affluent lifestyle are reflected in this 1915 photo. A Model T Ford is parked in the driveway while canoers return from a leisurely boat ride with their dog in tow. (Historical Association of Southern Florida)*

V 419
B NOV 18

◄ *An aviation base in Pensacola around 1918. (Pace Library—University of West Florida)*

News of the impending construction of the Panama Canal stimulated an enthusiastic movement to bring in additional railroads from the hinterland and take advantage of the new water routes to make Pensacola a more diversified port. When the potential of the automobile began to be recognized, Pensacolans—like other Floridians—looked to the highways. Four years before Carl Fisher launched his motorcade on the Dixie Highway, S.R. Mallory Kennedy drove from Pensacola to Chicago to demonstrate the possibilities of a highway connection from the Great Lakes to the Gulf. Despite the formidable obstacles imposed by Pensacola's location amid bays and lagoons that would require expensive bridging, local boosters encouraged cooperation with other cities across north Florida and the southern part of the nation to build a transcontinental highway. The Old Spanish Trail Association was formed in 1915 to do for that route what Fisher's Dixie Highway Association was doing for the north–south artery. Despite the optimism of the association's advocates, it would be some time before automobile roads would connect Pensacola with her neighbors to the east.

Good Roads and Grants-in-Aid

The automobile age was on its way. In response to the overtures of the Florida "Good Roads Association," which had been holding annual meetings since the late 1890s, the legislature created the state road department in 1915. The following year the U.S. Congress passed the Federal Highway Act to further a system of national highways. Its major feature was the appropriation of funds to be granted to the states on a matching basis. Florida was soon embarked on a program of road construction that transformed the state after World War I.

The Naval Air Station

While Pensacola's leaders searched for an economic vehicle suitable for a progressive city, one came inauspiciously in 1914. On the site of the old navy yard that had been closed in 1911, the naval air station—first called the Aeronautic Station—was opened after successful lobbying by C. E. Dobson and others. Assistant Secretary of the Navy Franklin D. Roosevelt visited Pensacola in 1913 and made a favorable report; a training camp was moved there shortly afterward. The advent of World War I soon accelerated the role of the new air station, and it has continued to expand ever since.

The Man from Alabama

The Old Spanish Trail Association was still talking about a highway when peninsular Florida was introduced to the panhandle by a most unusual politician. Sidney Catts had moved from Alabama to DeFuniak Springs in 1911 to be pastor of a Baptist church and to work as a traveling salesman. During his travels about the state, he perceived a feeling of discontent among many of the ordinary citizens with whom he came into contact and decided to do something about it.

Since regaining control from the Republicans in 1877, the white leaders of the state, acting through the Democratic party, had established a rigid "white supremacy." The racial structure remained firmly intact while the goals of the party changed markedly as new leaders succeeded older ones. Broward and his

▲ In his 1917 inaugural parade, newly elected Governor Sidney Catts, the "Cracker messiah," paid tribute to the automobile that took him around the state allowing him to reach voters in rural, out-of-the way villages. (Florida State Archives)

▼ A 1916 view of the Bagdad Railroad Line. Lines such as this one not only provided travelers with increased mobility but also allowed businesses to ship their supplies from inland to the coastal regions. (Pace Library—University of West Florida)

▲ Flight instructors
pose at a Miami base
in 1917. The leather
jacket, helmet, and
goggles are worn by a
member of the Jannus
family, possibly Roger,
the brother of Tony
Jannus. The Jannus
brothers worked as
pilots for the St. Peters-
burg-Tampa Airboat
Line, the first scheduled
commercial airline.
(Historical Association
of Southern Florida)

▲ Thomas Edison, one
of Florida's most
famous transplants,
visits the Key West

Naval Base during
World War I. (Florida
State Archives)

▲ *By 1917, Miami
provided residents and
visitors with bus service
to its outlying suburbs.
These sailors could
travel round-trip from
Miami to Coconut
Grove for only twenty-
five cents. (Historical
Association of Southern
Florida)*

allies, for example, had carried out a program that expanded the scope of government far beyond that which their Bourbon predecessors had considered sufficient. They had even implemented the primary nominating election to permit white voters a greater role in selecting candidates for office. But as time passed, many citizens began to believe that the nominating process had once again become dominated by a handful of party leaders. Since the Republican party had long since been eliminated as a serious opponent of the Democrats, people felt they had little real choice in the democratic process. However ill-defined, it was this dissatisfaction that Sidney Catts perceived as he traveled around the state, and he conceived a way of capitalizing on it.

Jesus Christ, Sears and Roebuck, and Sidney Catts

A good speaker with an uninhibited demagogic style, Catts campaigned for governor in 1916 on an emotional platform that appealed to the baser instincts of the less-informed voters. Taking advantage of an anti-Catholic mood that had already appeared in the nation, he offered himself as the defender of native Floridians against "Romanism." In a state where a majority of counties had already outlawed the sale of liquor, he advocated prohibition. Along the Gulf Coast Catts offered fishermen relief from the recently enacted laws designed to protect shellfish. Most of all, however, he offered himself as the defender of the "little men" against corporations and establishment politicians such as Comptroller William V. Knott, his major opponent in the campaign.

Frequently displaying two large pistols on the speaker's platform, Catts declared them necessary to defend himself against those who wished to silence

▲ *A typical middle-class home owned by a Pensacola black family at the turn of the century. (Pace Library—University of West Florida)*

Joe McLane and the Black Society of Palm Beach

At the turn of the century when the Royal Poinciana and the Breakers hotels were the nucleus of the wealthy winter society of Palm Beach, there was an equally well-established social set that was integral to the more affluent one and yet entirely separate from it. The black waiters and maids who served the wealthy whites who wintered at Palm Beach lived in their own quarters, had their own social gatherings, and their own social calendar.

At a time when blacks were denied access to most employment, the service jobs at Palm Beach were much sought after. Good workers could spend the winter season at the Florida resort and move north to Saratoga Springs, New York, or Asbury Park, New Jersey, for the summer. A person who could provide access to such employment wielded considerable power and influence. During the early years of the twentieth century that person was Joe McLane.

The Marianna-born McLane moved to Jacksonville at an early age before going to work as a waiter for the Royal Poinciana. He became headwaiter about 1910 and for more than twenty-five years provided employment for numerous black Floridians at the Palm Beach hotels as well as at Saratoga, Asbury Park, and Grand Central Station in New York City. While amassing a sizable fortune in Jacksonville real estate, McLane contributed generously to Edward Waters, Bethune-Cookman, and Memorial colleges. Nor did he forget his home town where he purchased a playground that is named for him. Some of the older black residents of Marianna proudly recall McLane's visits to his home town in his chauffeur-driven limousine.

▲Urging Floridians to "hurry," these Miami Red Cross nurses are promoting the purchase of World War I war bonds. (Historical Association of Southern Florida)

◀ A group of prisoners working a turpentine farm in Escambia County. This photo depicts one of the most noxious systems plaguing Florida. The convict lease system allowed prisoners to be rented by businesses with little regard for the workers' health and well-being. Most workers were black and incarcerated for crimes ranging from loitering to murder. Providing workers for unpopular jobs such as turpentining, this system yielded cheap labor for industry and regular revenue for the state. (Florida State Archives)

him, and he assured his listeners that they had only three dependable friends: Jesus Christ, Sears and Roebuck, and Sidney Catts. Traveling the back roads in a Model T and using a megaphone to deliver his speeches, Catts spread his word to many people who had rarely seen a candidate for office. They were apparently glad to see him.

Too Close to Call

Knott and the Democratic party officials had paid little attention to Catts until it was too late. With only a few votes separating them in the primary election, Knott and Catts sued and countersued until the party announced Knott as the winner by a bare majority. Unwilling to accept the result, Catts ran as an independent and defeated Knott in the general election, becoming the only candidate to defeat the regular Democratic nominee between 1876 and 1966.

A Turbulent Administration

Although he continued his demagogic tactics as governor, Catts pushed for a positive program that in many ways would have continued the progressivism of the Broward Era. He was unsuccessful in achieving most of his goals, however, because of the hostility of the opposition legislature, his habit of fighting with his supporters, and, most of all, the entry of the United States into World War I only a few weeks after his inauguration.

Florida Goes to War

America's brief participation in World War I slowed Florida's building boom somewhat but in the long run contributed to the runaway boom that followed the armistice. Thousands of young men went into the services and a sizable number served overseas. The state also became a training ground for many young men from other states. The navy expanded its air station at Pensacola, and flying schools were established at Miami and Arcadia. About 27,000 soldiers were stationed at Camp Johnston near Jacksonville, and smaller units spent several months at other locations. The navy established surface units for defense at Key West, Pensacola, and Tampa.

Large shipyards built vessels for the U.S. Shipping Board at Jacksonville and Tampa, and Florida's farmers responded to calls for increased food production. People willingly conserved scarce commodities and planted victory gardens. They worked with the Red Cross to make clothing and bandages and responded to the four Liberty Loan drives during the war. They were saddened by the casualty lists from the front and from the destructive influenza epidemic that swept the nation in 1918, but they turned out in great crowds to celebrate the armistice in November of that year.

The Other Side of Segregation

A severe labor shortage during the war emphasized the resurgence of a problem that many white Floridians preferred not to address. Blacks had been rigidly segregated by custom and law by the early twentieth century. Most were working as farm laborers or in the turpentine and lumber camps under varying conditions

▲ *In 1918, World War I volunteers stand at attention on the streets of Ocala. (Florida State Archives)*

◄ *A rare photograph of an early football team, representing the all-black Dunbar School in Quincy, Florida, about 1910. (Florida State Archives)*

◄ *Carrying the "separate but equal" ideology into every facet of society, Florida joined the rest of the United States in her segregation policies. Even railroad stations had segregated facilities, including separate waiting rooms for black and white customers. (Florida State Archives)*

The Grapefruit League

The Grapefruit League began in the early years of the twentieth century and was well established by the 1920s. It became traditional that Major League teams arrive in Florida for spring practice in March and play each other for the entertainment of local crowds. Although some of the players found the small Florida towns of the 1920s and 1930s quite limited in entertainment facilities, they appreciated the enthusiasm the locals showed for their spring games. As transportation improved and the Florida communities grew, spring training in the state became more popular among the players and the Grapefruit League competition became big business.

With the advent of radio and then television, Floridians were able to follow their favorite teams throughout the year, and many Major League players now make their homes in the state. None of this has detracted from the appeal of the Grapefruit League. On the contrary, it is becoming more important as cities strive to become the spring home of Major League teams and the business they bring. Kissimmee has attracted the Houston Astros with a handsome facility provided at public expense. Plant City has lured the Cincinnati Reds from Tampa, while St. Petersburg hopes to attract a team with its brand-new stadium. The Minnesota Twins have just left Orlando for the greener fields of Ft. Myers. The competition will undoubtedly continue.

All forms of spectator and competitive sports are part of modern Florida, but the venerable Grapefruit League seems still to be holding its own. ➤

---

of employment, but all were denied recourse to the law. Despite the repressive conditions, a few black professionals had developed thriving black communities in Jacksonville, Pensacola, Tampa, and a few of the smaller cities. Negro Boards of Trade, Miami's Negro Uplift Association, a few black labor unions, the churches, and black newspaper editors advocated law and order, thrift, hard work, and self-reliance in a society almost completely separate from whites.

Who Will Support the Negro Men of Business?

The tenuous balance was upset when the war interrupted immigration from Europe. Northern employers turned south and began recruiting blacks for the railroad, steel, and other heavy industries. During the next four years about 40,000 blacks left north Florida. Some went to Miami and other Southern cities, but most went to Northern states to work. Left without congregations, customers, or patients, many black ministers, businessmen, lawyers, and doctors went with them.

The National Colored Protective Association

Robert Randolph Robinson, a long-time black leader of Jacksonville, organized the National Colored Protective Association to stem the exodus. He wrote Governor Catts that blacks preferred to remain in the South, but they also needed equal justice, cessation of the "rough treatment colored people have been receiving at the hands of public officers," and better wages to offset the recent rise in the cost of living. Catts agreed to address an assembly of blacks and assured them that he would seek fair treatment for them. But he also called for unity on the basis of white supremacy and black inferiority. Whether the strange coalition between Robinson and Catts might have succeeded remains an unknown.

◄ *Members of the Pensacola Athletic Club, 1900. Although much of society believed participation in most sports was unladylike, this notion obviously did not hamper the enthusiasm of these women. The equipment shown in this photograph represents the variety of sports played by aspiring female athletes. (Pensacola Historical Society)*

◄ *A Lewis Hine photo of some of the young boys who worked in Tampa's renowned cigar factories in Ybor City. (Kuhn Library— University of Maryland)*

The exodus of blacks from Florida's farms and forests coincided with accelerating demands for workers in the war effort. Employers of blacks in Florida resented the U.S. Employment Service and the Bureau of Negro Economics, each of which they regarded as an intruder. The rising anger of the Florida employers coincided with the end of the war, the return of thousands of servicemen, and a rising tide of racial hostility and violence throughout the nation.

Governor of All of the People Some of the Time

Governor Catts had promised to represent all of the people of Florida, and he had supported Raymond Robinson's efforts to keep blacks from leaving the state. But when employers across the state asked Catts to help rid them of the U.S. government agents whom they believed to be threatening the status quo, the governor sided with them and lamented that "war conditions have so changed the negroes in the South." He even defended two lynch mobs who killed blacks in 1919.

A Most Liberal City for Colored People

Writing as editor of the *New York Age* in 1919, Jacksonville-born James Weldon Johnson commented that his native city had just had its first lynching. He noted that for many Jacksonville had been "a most liberal city for colored people," and he hoped that the violence was an exception. Six weeks later, however, Johnson wrote that terrorism was rising and that "a number of leading colored men of [Jacksonville] have been notified that they must go." When R. E. S. Toomey, a Miami attorney, led a delegation of the Negro Uplift Association to address the legislature that same year, it was denied a hearing because its petition was signed by blacks using such titles as Doctor, Mrs., and Reverend.

Two Ways of Life

The end of the war signaled a period of phenomenal growth in Florida. Populations and property values grew by leaps and bounds. The excitement of the boom overshadowed the plight of the state's black citizens, most of whom languished in a subservient, shadowy role for many more years.

▲ *Jacksonville in 1903 bore little resemblance to the city devastated by fire two years earlier. This is a view of Forsyth Street near the intersection of Laura Street. The building on the left with the tower is the Post Office, which survived the fire. In 1913, the utility lines were placed underground. (Florida State Archives)*

The White Primary

The primary election system enacted during the Broward Era was "democratic" only in a special sense. After the Republican party lost much of its membership in the late nineteenth century, it lost the chance of winning general elections. Since the Democratic nominees were assured of winning, the primary election was touted as a way for the people to have a voice in choosing their officials.

But it was also a way to eliminate black voters from the political process. At its 1900 convention, the Democratic party decided that only white people could be members of the party. According to the 1911 primary law, only party members could vote in the primary election. Blacks could still vote in the general election, but that was meaningless since there was no serious opposition party. One of the progressive reforms of the Broward Era consequently had the effect of eliminating black citizens from the political process until the U.S. Supreme Court outlawed the "white primary" in 1944.

▲ *Enjoying the famous wide beaches of east Florida, people gather at the "bathing hour"* *on the sands of Seabreeze, 1904. Socializing by the water added to the pleasures* *of life in this tropical paradise. (Florida State Archives)*

▼ *The* Metamora *steamer docked at Silver Springs on the Oklawaha River, 1900.* *(Florida State Archives)*

◀ *Women worked hard on Florida's farms. Feeding her brood of chickens was just one of the many chores this woman would perform in a normal workday. Photograph taken in 1915. (Tampa-Hillsborough County Public Library)*

▶ *The rough structures and dirt streets of Frostproof, Florida, contrast sharply with the electric poles and automobiles. (Florida State Archives)*

◀ *The ostrich plumes worn in the hats of fashionable women during the early 1900s made ostrich farming a novel but lucrative business. This ostrich-driven wagon from a Jacksonville ostrich farm attracted tourists while advertising Oliver W. Jr.'s business. (Florida State Archives)*

▲ *This unusual-looking vehicle is a 1916 tractor used to pull a log team in the piney backwoods* *of Oldsmar. (Tampa-Hillsborough County Public Library)*

▼ *Farmers bring their cotton to be weighed at the local gin. (Pensa-cola Historical Society)*

▲ *Members of a Fourth of July parade pass in front of Oldsmar's*

Wayside Inn, 1919. (Tampa-Hillsborough County Public Library)

▲ *With the barracks in the background, members of the 1916 Battery A Coast Artillery stand at attention.*

The company was located at Fort Barrancas, Florida. (Pace Library—University of West Florida)

▲ *A Bull gas tractor patented in 1915. The mechanization of agriculture wrought important social and economic changes in Florida. (Florida State Archives)*

▶ *Bringing home the stark realities of child labor, photographer Lewis Hine shot this grim portrait of Tony Valenti, a four-year-old Tampa newsboy, in 1913. (Florida State Archives)*

▲ *Advising visitors not to "annoy the alligators," the Tampa Alligator Farms cashed in on Florida's tourism trade just before World War I. (Florida State Archives)*

Chapter 10

The Turbulent 1920s

1306

◄ *Florida's version of the Orient Express, the Florida East Coast Railway ran from New York to Key West and was known as the* *Havana Special. Here, passengers relax in the "Camaguey" lounge car. (Florida State Archives)*

▲ *Miami Beach was a favorite haunt for national figures such as Warren G. Harding. During a visit in January 1921, Harding demonstrated the politi-* *cian's guaranteed crowd pleaser of kissing babies while playing a round of golf. (Historical Association of Southern Florida)*

▲ *Revenue agents proudly exhibit a huge display of confiscated material used in operating an illegal still in west central Florida in the 1920s. (Tampa-Hillsborough County Public Library)*

*D*uring the decade following the First World War, Americans indulged in a frenzy of social experimentation and rejection of traditional values while launching one of the most expansive and most disastrous speculative binges in their history. It was a time of readjustment after the intensities and restrictions of wartime, of labor unrest, of the Red Scare and racial violence, of "flappers" and raccoon coats, of legal prohibition and illegal bootlegging, of automobiles, of runaway inflation, and, finally, of economic collapse. Florida was spared none of this. Although the railroads and the incipient automobile revolution of the prewar years had brought increased attention to the state, Florida was still largely rural at the beginning of the third decade of the twentieth century. But that was about to change.

The emotional letdown following Woodrow Wilson's crusade to make the world safe for democracy led many Americans to question traditional values, but that was not easy for most Floridians. The majority of them applauded the great moral crusade against John Barleycorn as they witnessed with varying degrees of dismay the bathtub gin, the speakeasies, and the bootlegging that reached epidemic proportions in the 1920s. They also applauded William Jennings Bryan's denunciations of Charles Darwin's theories and Bryan's assurance that the world dated from 4004 B.C. and wondered why critics poked fun at them for doing so. And many Floridians applauded the Ku Klux Klan as the defender of traditional values while others condemned it as a bastion of bigotry. They watched in confusion as business profits soared while farmers struggled with plunging agricultural prices. Their world was changing, and while many found the changes unwelcome, they were unable to ignore them for long.

An Affair with the Automobile

The telephone, electric power, and many other technological advances were transforming Florida and bringing it closer to the rest of the nation, but nothing equaled the importance of the automobile. As the cities developed skylines with high-rise hotels, banks, and even department stores, the automobile made them more accessible. People began traveling to the cities and larger towns to take advantage of more varied entertainment and better shopping opportunities and to conduct business that had once been transacted by mail. Just beginning in the 1920s, this phenomenon signaled a major transformation and the decline of many of Florida's smaller communities. The transition from an overwhelmingly rural to an increasingly urban population was under way, and it was accelerated by the runaway real estate boom that reached its zenith in 1925.

The Tin Can Tourists

The automobile altered tourism as well. For years the railroads had been bringing wealthier visitors who wintered in Florida's balmy climate, but the automobile enabled people with more modest means to join the trek. The Dixie Highway and other roads invited families to pack their children and their tents into a Model T or comparable family car and head for the Sunshine State. These new visitors organized the "Tin Can Tourists of the World" at DeSoto Park in Tampa in 1919. The association held annual meetings thereafter at Tampa, Sarasota, and other Florida sites. They pitched their tents, organized games, and sometimes dismayed the host cities who might have preferred the more genteel visitors of an earlier day. But the automobiles continued to roll in and eventually made tourism a year-round enterprise since families with school-age children could travel more easily in the summer months.

It's June in Miami

It is impossible to say exactly why and when the Florida boom started. The prewar activities of John Collins, Carl Fisher, Walter Fuller, and others had undoubtedly sparked interest in Florida real estate. Word that the Firestones, the Fords, the Vanderbilts, Barron Collier, Roger Babson, T. Coleman Du Pont, Marshall Field, and other wealthy Americans were purchasing large Florida tracts certainly stimulated interest. But intensive advertising also played an important role. Probably no frontier area in the nation has ever been so widely advertised as Florida. The railroads tried to attract passengers and the hotels let their accommodations be known to potential tourists. The cities also advertised. Carl Fisher brought publicity to a new level when he purchased a huge illuminated sign at Times Square in New York. Its terse message that "It's June in Miami" must have been appealing to New Yorkers during the winter months. Pictures of bathing beauties enjoying white beaches and balmy waters permeated magazines and appeared on billboards all over the country. Once the visitor arrived in

▲ *Parked in the shade of a large oak, this home-built camper belonged to Irwin Speiran, a Canadian resident who first came to Florida in the late 1920s. Living in tourist camps, Speiran and his wife spent almost a year traveling around the state working at odd jobs, such as picking fruit, before returning to their northern home. Speiran never lost his fascination with Florida, returning yearly until his death in 1987. (Irwin Speiran Collection)*

▲ *Sporting a Mary
Pickford hairdo, Miss
Miami poses with a
Seminole chief, 1927.
(Historical Association
of Southern Florida)*

▲ Posing by a confiscated moonshine still, revenue agent James E. Bowdoin displays his catch in downtown Tallahassee. Moonshining was serious business, and the life of a revenuer was a dangerous one. Bowdoin was shot in 1924, two years after this photograph was taken, in west Florida. (Florida State Archives)

▼ Speaking from a trolley, William Jennings Bryan promotes Coral Gables real estate in the spring of 1926. (Historical Association of Southern Florida)

▲The Ku Klux Klan
enjoyed a period of
widespread popularity
in the 1920s. Here,
members of the Klan
march in Miami's

Fiesta of the American
Tropics Parade on
December 31, 1925.
(Florida State
Archives)

▼Promoting 100%
"Americanism," these
female Klan members
gather around a Betsy
Ross float as they
prepare to march in

Miami's 1927 Inde-
pendence Day Parade.
(Florida State
Archives)

Miami, he might witness the antics of Carl Fisher's elephants, but he would also see an attractive development on Miami Beach that had been scooped out of Biscayne Bay just a few years earlier. For Fisher the boom may have begun in 1923 when he sold $6 million worth of lots, but there was more to come.

Miami's Master Suburb

Among the almost countless schemers, dreamers, charlatans, promoters, and developers, there were many who, like Carl Fisher, fully intended to transform their ideas into action. "The best of the lot," according to historian Arva Parks, was George E. Merrick, who had arrived in south Florida as a boy in 1899. Having already completed several real estate ventures, Merrick launched his Coral Gables project in 1921 on a 3,000-acre tract that he intended to make "Miami's master suburb." He planned to adhere to a Mediterranean architectural style with wide streets interspersed with handsome plazas and tropical vegetation.

Because many thought that Coral Gables was too far out of the city, progress was slow during the first two years. Then, Miami real estate values began climbing and Coral Gables became a multimillion dollar project. As funds poured in, Merrick acquired waterfront property and built finger canals into Coral Gables. He spent more than $100 million on improvements and advertising. Full-page notices appeared in national newspapers and magazines. Branch offices were opened in Northern cities. Special Coral Gables cars were attached to Miami-bound trains, and Merrick's buses brought people from all over Florida and points beyond. Coral Gables had been catapulted into the big time by the increased interest in Florida real estate, which in turn helped accelerate the boom.

By 1925 wide boulevards had been completed, lakes and canals were carved out of the coral, a mountain was constructed to improve the flat landscape, two hundred miles of roads were paved, and the Biltmore Hotel and the Venetian waterways were completed. Schools, banks, and stores were built, all in conformity with the Mediterranean architectural standards. Although the project was only about one-fourth completed when the boom ended, some 1,500 private residences had been approved by the architectural board. Financial difficulties finally overwhelmed Merrick, but he did give Miami a "master suburb."

Dredging and Filling

The Shoreland Company did not experience the delay that Merrick had encountered. When the company advertised its Miami Shores development in December 1924, first-day sales amounted to $2.5 million. Within a few days, people were buying tracts that were still underwater on the promise that dredging was soon to begin. The company's Arch Creek sale outdid them all in September 1925. With 400 acres of loose sand for sale, the Shoreland offices opened at eight-thirty in the morning. When the office closed at eleven o'clock, $33 million had been collected. It took the bookkeeper five days to learn the land was oversubscribed by $11 million.

Addison Mizner

Henry Flagler had established Palm Beach as a resort for the wealthy when he

▲ *In 1928, Helen Keller (center) paid a visit to the Florida State College for Women (later known as Florida State University). (Florida State Archives)*

◀ *Catering to the influx of tourists, Florida's lakes and beaches provided bathhouses for the convenience of visitors such as those enjoying the waters of Lake Bradford, 1923. (Florida State Archives)*

◀ *In 1920, a leisurely drive over this narrow brick-paved road in Largo took motorists past orange groves and oaks draped with Spanish moss. (Florida State Archives)*

▶ *Erected in 1923 at the Lee-Hendry county line, this arch welcomed visitors to the sportsman's paradise and notified them of town distances. The wooden structure rotted away long ago. (Florida State Archives)*

built the Royal Poinciana and the Breakers. After the war wealthy people began building mansions instead of sojourning in hotels during the "season." The architect Addison Mizner arrived about that time as the guest of his friend, Paris Singer, who induced him to design and construct the Everglades Club. During the next few years, demands for Mizner's services increased as he gained a reputation for high standards and an eclectic Mediterranean architectural style. By 1923, Mizner was building expensive Palm Beach villas for the nation's wealthiest people. His involvement in the boom was inevitable.

With the backing of Singer, two of the Vanderbilt brothers, T. Coleman Du Pont, Irving Berlin, and others, Mizner announced his Boca Raton project in April 1925. First-day receipts exceeded $2 million as crowds jammed sales offices in both Miami and Palm Beach. Work began on a town that included a beachfront hotel, a casino, an air terminal, a yacht basin, and Irving Berlin's Cabaret. As Mizner's sales increased, several other projects were announced for Boca Raton. But it was too late. By September, sales amounted to more than $11 million, but continued success depended on the volume of future sales. As the boom slowed in late 1925, so did Mizner's project. He was obliged to surrender control to new managers, and the project was eventually liquidated in 1927.

The Eighth Wonder of the World

An increase in tourism followed the arrival of the Tin Can Tourists in 1921, and Tampa real estate began to change hands a little later. The catalyst for the boom, however, was the Davis Islands project, which began in late 1924. D. P. Davis had witnessed the construction of Miami Beach out of the bottom of Biscayne Bay and resolved to duplicate it at Tampa. Acquiring title to a spit of land and a marshy area in Tampa Bay known as Big Grassy and Little Grassy islands, Davis launched an advertising program and made plans for reclaiming the land. Calling his project the "Eighth Wonder of the World," Davis offered lots for sale in October 1925 even as dredges were scooping sand to create building sites. He sold out within the month for a total of about $18 million. Unaware that the boom was approaching its end, Davis moved to St. Augustine, where he planned to repeat his Tampa enterprise. As payments on his previous sales slowed in 1926, Davis ran out of resources. He died at sea later that year. It is still a matter of speculation whether he died by accident or by his own design. His Davis Island project was a lasting monument to his initiative, however, and remains a part of modern Tampa.

The Big Auction of the Season

Land prices rose all over the state, and many smaller communities such as Winter Haven had their own booms. Salesmen learned the methods of Doc Dammers and spectacular auctions became commonplace. A typical one was promoted by Mason Roberts near Orlando as "The Big Auction of the Season." He promised "Twin auctioneers . . . A band! A balloon ascension! A parachute drop!" And enthusiasm spread into the hinterland. Land values rose as far inland as Lake City and as far west as Pensacola. Thousands of acres of old plantation land were bought by wealthy individuals and converted into hunting preserves.

▲ *Buses bringing potential investors to view development property line the spacious street in front of the Coral Gables administration building. (Historical Association of Southern Florida)*

◄ *Promotion of Florida encouraged unique and novel ideas, and what could be more camp than an elephant caddy? Miami Beach, 1923. (Historical Association of Southern Florida)*

► *Coral Gables land developer George Merrick speaks to a crowd of potential investors. (Historical Association of Southern Florida)*

► *In the Venice of the South, gondolas line the Collins Canal as passengers glide past the watery piazzas. (Historical Association of Southern Florida)*

◀ *Polo, the sport of princes, being played on the grounds of one of Miami Beach's exclusive hotels. (Historical Association of Southern Florida)*

▶ *Nestled among the Tampa Bay Hotel advertising billboard, the Oaks Restaurant, and the Green Gables Tourist Camp, Jack's Place sold Coca-Cola, Orange Crush, and hamburgers and hot dogs to Hillsborough County visitors in the 1920s. (Tampa-Hillsborough County Public Library)*

◀ *Members of the Cleveland Indians before a game during spring training in Lakeland, 1924. The Grapefruit League blossomed during the 1920s. (Florida State Archives)*

▶ *Automobiles line Park Avenue in Winter Park in 1925, indicating a prosperous and growing Florida boom town. (Florida State Archives)*

▲ *Whether playing cards or shuffleboard, winter residents found St. Petersburg a retire-* *ment haven. (Tampa-Hillsborough County Public Library)*

▲ *Well-known golf legends Bobby Jones (left) and Walter Hagen play golf at St. Peters-* *burg's Pasadena Golf Course in 1926. (Tampa-Hillsborough County Public Library)*

▲ *Boxing great Jack Dempsey displays his golfing form to Miami admirers. (Historical Association of Southern Florida)*

▲ *During the heyday of stock market investing, M. J. Meehan and Company serviced guests at Miami Beach's Breakers Hotel. (Historical Association of Southern Florida)*

The Gateway to Florida

Although Jacksonville was affected by the speculative boom and Telfair Stockton drained and reclaimed marsh land for development, that city grew most dramatically because of its continuing role as the gateway to Florida. The new Barnett National Bank building was only one of the skyscrapers that dotted the skyline along the river. The St. Johns River Bridge earned huge revenues from the flood of automobile traffic. Perhaps the most dramatic evidence of growth was the Florida East Coast Railroad terminal, which was expanded in 1924. The new facility was outgrown before it was completed. With another expansion in 1925, it was again overwhelmed by freight and passenger traffic by the time construction was finished.

The Binder Boys and the Beginning of the End

With land changing hands repeatedly—Walter Fuller reported one parcel that was sold and resold ten times in thirteen days—at increasing prices, the speculative boom became dependent on a continuing supply of new buyers. It also invited a new breed of speculator. It was the "binder boys" who eventually gave Florida real estate a bad name. Since about thirty days were required to complete the necessary paperwork on a land sale, these enterprising individuals bought "binders," usually amounting to deposits of ten percent, with the intention of reselling them before ever having to put up the remainder of the sale price. Eventually, binders were sold over and over again with the price increasing at each transaction. Such a procedure was bound to bring disaster.

Bedlam and Chaos

By the fall of 1925, Miami was a crowded, noisy place where beds were being rented in shifts. The cost of living was exorbitant, and milling crowds blocked sidewalks and hampered construction crews at work on dozens of skyscrapers. The Florida East Coast Railroad was bringing in about two thousand passengers each day, and few were leaving on northbound trains. The highway between St. Augustine and Palatka was made one-way southbound during daylight to ease the traffic jam. On September 27, 1925, the infamous Ashley gang staged a breakout for one of its members incarcerated in the Dade County jail. The getaway went awry and shots were fired. No one noticed because the noise of nearby construction drowned out the shooting.

Each arriving train was met by the "binder boys" waving their paper property and imploring the new arrivals to buy before it was too late. Some bought and others waited, but property continued to change hands. Buyers were unconcerned about prices because they expected to sell immediately at even higher prices. Additional sales by the thousands were being made in land offices all over the country. An agent in Waterbury, Connecticut, sold 1,600 parcels of Florida land. The fury of speculation could not last.

The Railroad Embargo and the *Prinz Valdemar*

Trouble was already on the way. On August 18, 1925, the Florida East Coast Railroad embargoed freight cars of other lines. It was a temporary measure to

◄ *This sign advertises the dream of automobile tycoon Ransom E. Olds. In 1917, he bought nearly 60 square miles of land on the east banks of north Pinellas County, planning a farming community for his retired factory* workers. Although he sold out in 1923 to Harold Prettyman, this 1925 poster still advertised the colony of Oldsmar as a "demonstration farm worth visiting." (Florida State Archives)

► *Under the eaves of the Christina Railroad Station promoters unfurl a new "city for colored people" in 1925. (Florida State Archives)*

◄ *In 1926, John D. Rockefeller visited the fair sponsored by the Ormond Beach Women's Club. Countless Floridians remember receiving dimes from the "Robber Baron." (Florida State Archives)*

► *Visitors to Florida in the 1920s could stop at roadside fruit stands, such as Floyd's near Miami, and purchase the coveted citrus to send back to their friends up north. (Florida State Archives)*

Public Enemy Number One

With rumrunners regarded almost as folk heroes, speakeasies operating around the clock, and gambling and horseracing becoming favorite pastimes, Miami began attracting a new kind of tourist in the late 1920s, and some of them stayed on as permanent residents. Al Capone first arrived in 1928 and rented the top floor of the Ponce de Leon Hotel for the winter. He liked the place so well that he purchased a mansion on Palm Island. An ambivalent Miami watched while Capone put on several bashes. Some wanted to invite him to join the country club while others wanted to run him out of town. Alarmed at what gangsters might do to the state's reputation, Governor Doyle Carlton declared Capone an "undesirable" and ordered sheriffs to arrest him on sight. Capone's lawyers obtained an injunction restraining the state from such action. He left the state unmolested but was arrested and imprisoned for several months in Pennsylvania for carrying a gun.

Back in Florida in 1930, Capone was welcomed by a newspaper crusade against him and authorities tried to close his Palm Island home as a public nuisance. That failing, civic leaders sought to bring him to trial for illegal activities. But that also proved impossible when it became clear that countless businesses were guilty of the same things of which Capone was being accused. The federal government provided a partial solution by imprisoning the gangster for income tax evasion during most of the 1930s. He returned to Palm Island a sick and broken man in 1939 and lived eight more years. After his death, the Capone family was rarely heard from until 1965, when Al junior was convicted of shoplifting $3.80 worth of merchandise from a local supermarket.

relieve the backlog on the Miami sidetracks where 850 freight cars were waiting to be unloaded. With another 150 freight cars backed up at Jacksonville and at least 700 more on the way, railroad officials felt something had to be done. The embargo was extended to cover the entire state in late October and was not finally lifted until early 1926.

All kinds of surface vessels were pressed into service to bring in supplies. Then, in January 1926, the *Prinz Valdemar*, which was under renovation to become a floating cabaret, slipped its moorings and capsized in the channel. For more than a month nothing moved in or out of the harbor. Construction crews were dismissed and unfinished skyscrapers marked the Miami skyline.

A Siege of Bad Press

The enthusiasm for Florida investments waned about the time the transportation difficulties set in. The National Better Business Bureau, the Florida Real Estate Commission, and the Florida Association of Real Estate Boards received thousands of complaints about fraudulent sales practices. Many exposés appeared in national magazines. The Scripps-Howard newspaper chain published a series of critical articles in September 1925 and tersely announced that the boom was over. A newspaper in Columbus, Ohio, carried a full-page advertisement from the city's bankers, cautioning against buying Florida land. The Richmond, Virginia, city council discussed passage of an ordinance forbidding migration to Florida. A newspaper in Asheville, North Carolina, called for martial law in the peninsular state. The *New York Times* agreed with bankers in the Northern states who were protesting the enormous volume of withdrawals from their institutions for investment in Florida real estate.

The Truth about Florida

Governor John W. Martin and a group of Floridians countered the adverse publicity by inviting editors and publishers to a meeting at the Waldorf Astoria Hotel in New York to learn the "truth about Florida." New projects were announced. Hugh Anderson and Roy Wright of the Shoreland Company paid $30,000 an acre for the Deering Estate and announced plans for its development as Bay Plaza. Joseph Young announced the opening of his $3 million Hollywood Hotel, and Glen Curtis revealed plans for Opa-Locka, which he intended to build around an *Arabian Nights* theme. The social season opened in December 1925 with a huge reception. Rachel Jane Hamilton appeared in concert and Arthur Pryor's band played for the dance. The king of Greece made a well-publicized visit in early January. Gene Tunney was selling real estate and Red Grange came to put on a football exhibition.

The Supply of Suckers Has Run Out

Despite the counterattack, the speculative boom was over. Real estate sales declined sharply in February 1926. Bank deposits dropped and some institutions began calling in loans. Buyers failed to make payments on their purchases, and even responsible developers such as George Merrick and Addison Mizner were forced into default. There are many explanations of the collapse of the boom: the transportation problems of late 1925, the adverse publicity throughout the nation, a sharp decline in the stock market, and reports that the Internal Revenue Service was looking into the huge profits. Walter Fuller's cruder explanation was that "the supply of suckers has run out." With buyers constantly driving up prices in expectation of even higher resales, confidence must have been eroded by the many warnings appearing in late 1925. As doubt increased, the number of buyers declined.

▲ *Named for Florida cities, these Florida Airways passenger planes await their next flight at Tampa's Drew Field, 1928. (Tampa-Hillsborough County Public Library)*

Hurricanes

More adversity was on the way. As if to add nature's disapproval of the frenzied last days of the boom, a giant hurricane struck Miami on September 17, 1926. At that time no one knew much about hurricanes, but when the wind instruments blew away at 124 miles per hour, there was little doubt about what had happened. The wind blew through the night and then subsided. Not realizing they were in the eye of the storm, people went outside to survey the damage. When the wind struck from the other direction, many were killed or injured. Nearly 400 people died and more than 6,000 were injured. About 47,000 were homeless. Some 2,000 homes were destroyed and 3,000 more were damaged. The property loss in Miami alone was estimated at about $20 million. President Calvin Coolidge appealed for aid, and a generous nation responded with nearly $4 million. The Cuban government sent several thousand dollars and 50,000 complete typhoid inoculations.

Almost exactly two years later, on September 16, 1928, an even stronger storm—measured at 130 miles per hour—struck Palm Beach and forced the

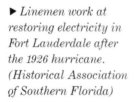 *Following the destruction of the 1926 hurricane, Mrs. A. O. Weeks of Dania finds little privacy in what remains of her once-modern bathroom. (Historical Association of Southern Florida)*

▶ *Linemen work at restoring electricity in Fort Lauderdale after the 1926 hurricane. (Historical Association of Southern Florida)*

▲ *Left with nothing but a counter, a few chairs, and a menu board, employees of the South Andrews Cafe in Fort Lauderdale pose amidst the damage left by the 1926 hurricane. (Historical Association of Southern Florida)*

▼ *Before air-conditioned schools, teachers often held class outside to escape the heat of enclosed areas. This Miami teacher and her students enjoy their open-air classroom. (Historical Association of Southern Florida)*

waters of Lake Okeechobee over its earthen dike, flooding Pahokee, Belle Glade, and other communities south of the big lake. An estimated 2,000 lives were lost, but the count remained inexact because bodies had to be buried in mass graves to avoid the spread of epidemic diseases.

The Stock-Buying Frenzy and National Economic Collapse

What had happened to Florida land values was happening to national stock prices in the latter 1920s. People were buying stock on margin and then borrowing to buy more stock. All were gambling on the prospects of ever-increasing prices. The stock market sagged in 1927 but quickly rallied partly because President Calvin Coolidge declared the business of the country entirely sound. A major business leader declared it every American's duty to become rich. By 1929 price indexes had doubled from their 1927 highs. Then, in late October, it all came tumbling down. Within two weeks about 40 percent of the paper wealth of the nation had been wiped out. The collapse of the stock market and the underlying imbalances in the national and world economies left the nation wallowing in depression for years.

Progress Had Been Expensive

Floridians were already feeling financial adversity and not just from the collapse of the real estate boom. Governor Martin became known as Florida's road building governor. Indeed, more than 2,200 miles of state roads had been completed between 1925 and 1929. The opening of the Tamiami Trail in 1928 was celebrated as the centerpiece of Martin's program. Barred by a constitutional provision against debt, the state had emerged from the building program without many outstanding obligations. But that was not the case with the cities, counties, and special taxing districts. As the state grew in the 1920s, so had confidence in the future. Local governments borrowed heavily to expand services such as streets, water supplies, sewage disposal, and schools. As revenues declined in the latter years of the decade, these entities began defaulting on their obligations. Since they were statutory creations of the state, Florida was ultimately responsible for the debts. As the fourth decade of the twentieth century approached,

▲ *A 1920s Wauchula turpentine still. (Florida State Archives)*

The Mediterranean Fruit Fly

It must have seemed in 1929 that everything that could possibly go wrong had done so. That was not the case. An infestation of the Mediterranean fruit fly was discovered in a grove south of Orlando in April of that year. A concerted effort was quickly launched by the U.S. Department of Agriculture, the University of Florida Extension Service, and private individuals to combat the infestation. Shipments of most fruit, vegetables, and foliage plants were prohibited, and the National Guard enforced the quarantine over a huge area of central Florida. At a cost of nearly $7 million, the loss of a year's production, and the destruction of hundreds of acres of infected groves, the fruit fly was finally brought under control by late 1930. Annual fruit production had been reduced by about one-third, and many foliage growers were driven out of business never to recover. ➤

◀ *Employees of Perry's Burton Swartz Cypress Company pose on this 3,000-year-old cypress, 1926. A strong belief that man should conquer nature and prosper from the victory doomed these giant trees. (Florida State Archives)*

▼ *Black field workers cut sugar cane near Sopchoppy around 1926. (Florida State Archives)*

▶ *Employees at the Delores Brickyard, located along the Escambia River near Molino, pose in front of the company's brick kiln, 1920s. (Florida State Archives)*

◀ *A 1924 photo of a dynamite drill rig used to place dynamite underground. Explosives were needed to blast the hard limestone rock of the surface ground. These rigs were used in building the Tamiami Trail between the east and west Florida coasts. (Florida State Archives)*

Governor Doyle Carlton's administration looked gloomily at its declining revenues, increasing demands for assistance from hungry people, and a mushrooming volume of defaulted local debt.

Two Booms and One Bust

After soaring to the heights of prosperity and beyond in the first half of the 1920s, Floridians had dropped to the depths of depression by 1930. The speculative boom and its collapse had caused serious losses for many and a disrupted economy for most. Yet underneath the speculation, there had been substantial growth that wrought permanent changes in the state. The permanent population had grown by half. Tourism was now an established industry no longer limited to the wealthy but augmented by middle class owners of automobiles. All that was obscured for a while by the Great Depression that gripped the state and nation in the 1930s.

▲ *The elegant Morocco Pool served as the centerpiece of the 1920s Temple Terrace Country Club. Today, Florida College occupies these buildings. (Tampa-Hillsborough County Public Library)*

▲ *During the heyday of early filmmaking, Florida rivaled Hollywood in movie production. This 1920s film crew,* with cameras mounted on a biplane, prepares to shoot aerial scenes. (Florida Endowment for the Humanities)

▼ *Florida's beaches provide an Arabic backdrop for this unknown* film, c. 1920. (Historical Association of Southern Florida)

◀ *During the 1920s, the Seminole tribe of south Florida became one of the state's biggest tourist attractions. This photo reflects the result of cross-cultural exchange. The woman has retained the Seminole tradition of adding strands of beads for important events in her life (e.g., birthdays, marriage) while adopting a hairstyle influenced by Anglo culture. It was the habit of white Floridians, as well as a style of the period, to wear hats as protection from the sun. Seminole women adapted this fashion by cutting pieces of cardboard into brimlike shapes and weaving their hair around the form to fashion a hairstyle similar to a hat. (Historical Association of Southern Florida)*

▲ *Seminole Indian "Alligator Sam" teaches his young students the art of archery. (Historical Association of Southern Florida)*

▼ *A Seminole Indian family gathers around the campfire where food is being prepared. (Historical Association of Southern Florida)*

◀ *Before the live action of television, sportscasters had to be more inventive in holding the attention of their audiences. Jacksonville's newspaper, the* Florida Times Union, *set up a platform in the street and provided a play-by-play report of the World Series match between the St. Louis Cardinals and Philadelphia Athletics. (Florida State Archives)*

▶ *Alachua County Confederate veterans gather on the steps of the county courthouse in Gainesville, November 4, 1925. (Florida State Archives)*

◀ *Near La Belle, churchgoers congregate on the banks of the Caloosahatchee, near the Homer Hand Boat Shop, to witness a baptizing by Reverend Oscar Roberts. (Florida State Archives)*

◀ *Members of the Lake City Police Department, led by Chief of Police Charlie Eaton (center). (Florida State Archives)*

▶ *The Tamiami Service Station, located at 100 N.W. Second Street in Miami, 1924. (Historical Association of Southern Florida)*

◀ *Auto racing enjoyed a popular following on the wide beaches of Florida's east coast. On February 25, 1929, Sir Henry Segrave's racer "Golden Arrow" set a world speed record of 231 miles per hour at Daytona Beach. (Florida State Archives)*

▶ *On call and ready for action, members of a 1920s Pensacola fire department await their next emergency summons. (Pace Library—University of West Florida)*

◄ *Florida's wilderness environment provided tourists as well as residents with an abundance of wildlife for hunting. These men proudly display their trophy after a successful bear hunt in Wakulla County, 1929. (Florida State Archives)*

◄ *The abundance of game kept Florida's tourist hotels stocked with fresh meat and contributed to the state's reputation as a hunter's paradise. These men are returning from a successful turkey hunt. (Tampa-Hillsborough County Public Library)*

Chapter 11

Depression and
Renewal in the
1930s

◄ *Unable to find work in their native state of Missouri, a migrant packing-house worker (digging in the dirt) and his family look for better times in Florida. Discouraged and disillusioned, he succinctly summed up their predicament: "We never lived like hogs before, but we sure does now." Canal Point, 1939. (Florida State Archives)*

▲ *Franklin D. Roosevelt greets Floridians from the "Presidential" car of the Atlantic Coast Line Railway, 1930s. (Historical Association of Southern Florida)*

▲ *Likened to social security, the Townsend Plan was one of the more popular schemes to end the plunging incomes of depression-wracked Americans. This billboard in Frost-proof urged residents to accept the plan that would provide "business recovery." (Florida State Archives)*

*W*ith tax delinquencies and business failures increasing, banks closing, and hungry people seeking relief from local governments with empty treasuries, Floridians responded to Governor Doyle Carlton's request to tighten their belts in 1931. Cities reduced tax millage and cut salaries. Chambers of commerce asked merchants to give good prices to residents willing to undertake home-improvement projects to keep people working. "Buy now" campaigns were launched. The Dade County Welfare Board campaigned for "a penny a day" to help the hungry. The city of Jacksonville appropriated money for public works and hired unemployed men to work three days per week. The Community Chest raised funds for a soup kitchen that fed hundreds of people. Alfred Du Pont, who had invested heavily in Jacksonville, donated money to put unemployed men to work on city parks. Many other communities organized charitable agencies as the demands of the needy exhausted the resources of traditional private relief. The 1931 legislature authorized parimutuel wagering at horse and dog tracks and earmarked half of the proceeds for counties in an effort to ease the financial situation. But at the same time a committee on unemployment recommended that Governor Carlton notify the president that the state would take care of its own problems. The committee turned out to be wrong.

Beyond Self-Help

As one local agency after another exhausted its resources and Governor Carlton announced that the state was unable to meet the emergency, it seemed that some outside assistance was imperative. There was no precedent for national action and President Herbert Hoover was reluctant to set one, but the scope of the problem finally caused the president to ask for emergency legislation. In 1932 Congress created the Reconstruction Finance Corporation to make emergency loans to financial institutions enabling them to support job-producing private projects. Its authority was soon expanded to include loans to state and local governments for public works projects. The agency eventually loaned billions of dollars, but this was only one of many federal programs of the 1930s.

A New Deal

When the American people elected Franklin Delano Roosevelt as president in 1932 on his vague promise of "a new deal for the American people," they could have had little idea of what that entailed. The program evolved helter-skelter in response to the nation's needs as envisioned by the president and Congress over the next few years. Welcomed by a people alarmed at the plight in which they found themselves, the New Deal programs were generally regarded as emergency measures justified by the immense scope of the nation's problems. In fact, the development of positive national governmental programs in response to immediate problems made permanent changes in the relations between national and state governments on the one hand and between governments at all levels and individual citizens on the other. The array of alphabet agencies spawned in the depression influenced the lives of Americans in ways unheard of in earlier times and stimulated comparable action on the part of state and local governments. The cumulative effect was to provide much more public assistance to individuals while circumscribing the range of choices traditionally left to them in social and economic matters.

The Needs of the Moment

Only a few dissenters at the time thought of the long-range implications of the new programs. Most people were concerned with immediate conditions rather than theories, and those conditions required drastic action. Building on the modest programs initiated by Herbert Hoover and adapting to the nation an emergency relief system he had implemented as governor of New York, Roosevelt obtained legislation creating the Federal Emergency Relief Administration (FERA), which provided funds to the states to finance public works that would create jobs. Supplementing the FERA as a direct relief operation was the Civil Works Administration (CWA). While some of its projects were later criticized as "make-work," its purpose was to get people on payrolls quickly as a way of infusing cash into the communities and regenerating the economy. The CWA was absorbed by the FERA in 1934, and direct relief was returned to the state and local governments. The Works Progress Administration (WPA) took over public works projects at the same time and continued them until the early 1940s. These agencies employed thousands of people, enabling them to feed themselves and their families and to salvage their self-respect.

While the human benefits of these programs can scarcely be exaggerated, they

▲ *Migrant vegetable pickers await their paycheck and ride back to their camp in Homestead, 1939. (Library of Congress)*

▼ *A family of migrant laborers gather in front of their makeshift home in Canal Point, 1939. (Florida State Archives)*

▲ *Bedraggled and dirty, this migrant family in Belle Glade symbolizes the hardships faced by many Americans striving to survive in the Great Depression. (Florida State Archives)*

also provided important physical facilities. City halls, county courthouses, playgrounds, lighted baseball fields and tennis courts, roads, bridges, and airfields were constructed all over the state. Public housing was built in Jacksonville, Tampa, and Miami. A levee was built around Lake Okeechobee, the inland waterway around the state was extended, and a cross-Florida canal was begun. School buildings were erected, teachers' salaries were supplemented, and unemployed teachers were hired to teach adults in night classes. Sewing rooms and canneries provided employment at the same time they taught valuable skills. Artists were employed to paint murals on public buildings and to teach art. Musicians were given jobs playing for the public, and a theatre project provided jobs for hungry actors who then provided free entertainment for the public.

Key West and the Overseas Highway

One of the most ambitious FERA undertakings was at Key West. Left stranded as the nation turned away from water transportation, the island city was isolated, debt-ridden, and desperate by 1934 when local authorities turned the community over to the federal agency. In cooperation with local citizens who pledged $1.5 million for a cleanup campaign, the FERA renovated the Casa Marina Hotel, arranged an annual festival, launched an advertising campaign, booked houses for rent, and set up ferry and airplane service to make Key West a tourist attraction. A companion project was the Overseas Road and Toll Bridge District, which received FERA assistance to build a highway from the mainland. Several hundred World War I veterans went to work, but the highway suffered a major setback on Labor Day, 1935, when a fierce hurricane struck and drowned more than four hundred workers. The storm damaged the Florida East Coast Railroad overseas extension so severely that it was abandoned and turned over to the highway agency. Work resumed and Key West was joined to the mainland by a highway in 1938.

The Attempted Assassination of FDR

On February 15, 1933, a large crowd was gathered at the Bayfront Park band shell in Miami to hear an address by president-elect Franklin D. Roosevelt. On the bandstand with Roosevelt was Chicago Mayor Anton Cermak, who was busily trying to ingratiate himself with Roosevelt after having unsuccessfully supported his opponent during the recent campaign. Roosevelt had not uttered a full sentence before Giuseppe Zangara, an unemployed bricklayer, began firing a cheap pistol he had purchased from a local pawnshop. Five people were wounded in the melee, including Mayor Cermak, who was standing only about a foot from Roosevelt. Zangara was arrested and, within a week, tried and sentenced to eighty years in prison. Then, Cermak unexpectedly died from his wounds. Zangara was indicted for murder, tried, convicted, and executed within thirty-three days after his attempted assassination of the president-elect.

Some writers have speculated that the attempted assassination was actually aimed at Cermak by mobsters who wanted him out of the way. Most authorities point out, however, that the Chicago mayor was on good terms with the mob leaders at the time and that Zangara really was trying to kill Roosevelt. ➤

◀ *Gathering her children for a sparse meal of bread and milk, this mother, wife of a migrant worker, provides what care she can under extremely adverse conditions. (Florida State Archives)*

▶ *With his family's most important possession parked in front of their tin shack, a migrant laborer's child explores his temporary home. (Florida State Archives)*

◀ *Lacking even the conveniences of "Tin Can Tourists," these children of Belle Glade migrant workers live in squalid conditions. (Florida State Archives)*

Roosevelt's Tree Army

One of the most popular New Deal agencies was the Civilian Conservation Corps (CCC), which was aimed at salvaging two of the nation's most important resources: its youth and its natural environment. Youths from families on relief were paid thirty dollars per month—most of which was sent to their families—to perform wholesome tasks that taught them useful skills. Young men from all over the state and many parts of the nation were assigned to about two dozen camps in Florida. They provided fire protection and built roads in the national and state forests, and helped originate the state park system by completing or doing substantial work on the new state parks. They cooperated with the Florida Forest Service in planting millions of pine seedlings on thousands of acres of cutover land that had been left idle and virtually worthless by the lumber companies. Many of the seedlings were planted on private lands as well as on acreage belonging to the state and the nation. Many of the roads, trails, and recreational facilities in Osceola, Ocala, and Apalachicola national forests were built by CCC men. Highland Hammock, Myakka River, Gold Head Branch, O'Lena, Fort Clinch, Florida Caverns, and Hillsborough River were among the state parks that the CCC either began or substantially improved. CCC men also built Greynolds and Matheson Hammock parks in Dade County and St. Marks Wildlife Refuge.

The Second New Deal

While the FERA and other earlier New Deal legislation was aimed at relief for a nation of needy people and their myriad programs tempered the effects of the depression, other laws addressed the longer-range need for reform. Based on the assumption that the economic life of the nation had become so complicated that individuals were sometimes affected by events beyond their control, an array of new laws made the national and state governments responsible for a broad range of social programs. Adhering to the principles of federalism, the new laws usually involved funding by the national government for programs to be administered by the states according to certain "guidelines." Although some Floridians were reluctant to see the national government assuming such an enhanced role in the state's affairs, Governor David Sholtz—an avid New Dealer—encouraged cooperation, and big government came to Florida in the mid-1930s.

Social Security

The most inclusive and sometimes the most controversial of these new laws was the Social Security Act of 1935, which established an annuity program to be funded by payroll taxes on individuals and their employers so that pensions would be available when workers reached retirement age. There was also provision for assistance to dependent children and an "old age" pension for those who had already reached retirement age. The latter was to be paid by matching funds from the U.S Treasury and the state. Critics argued that the creation of numbers for individual Social Security accounts would give "big brother" too much power. Proponents argued—somewhat erroneously, as it turned out—that Social Security numbers would never be used for any purpose other than the personal accounts.

◀ With a portrait of her friend Franklin D. Roosevelt reflected in the mirror, Mary Bethune Cookman is photographed in her office at the college that she founded. (Florida Historical Society)

◀ In 1937, at the age of ninety-three, Charity Steward has her photo taken. Born in 1844, Charity was a former slave who hid in the swamps and made soap for the soldiers in Jefferson County. When the Civil War ended, she returned to the home of her former owners, where she remained until their death. She then lived alone in a log cabin in Jefferson County for many years. (Florida State Archives)

The Townsend Plan and Old-Age Pensions

Since the state's participation in the "old-age" pension program required a constitutional amendment, there was an extended debate over it as well. Older people were well represented, however, by numerous Townsend Clubs. Dr. Francis Townsend of California had attracted attention by his plan for reviving the economy and ending the depression. Without mentioning a possible source of funds, Townsend called on the government to pay every American over age sixty a pension of $200 per month, provided only that recipients spent it all each month. Older people had seen great virtue in the plan and Townsend Clubs sprang up all over the nation, including Florida. When the Townsend plan failed to win support, the Townsend Clubs campaigned for the more modest pension plan. The constitutional amendment was approved and Florida began paying "old-age" pensions.

Beginning of Big Government

Despite its hesitant acceptance in the 1930s and the many changes in the program since, Social Security has become an accepted and essential part of life in modern Florida. Accompanied by numerous other beneficent and regulatory agencies, it brought big government to the state. By the late 1930s, new state agencies—sometimes, but not always, stimulated by national incentives—included a new social welfare board, a state planning board, an employment board, a park service, a conservation commission, a beverage department, a citrus commission, a milk commission, and state farmers' markets. A workmen's compensation act was passed, and the state assumed a greater responsibility for public schools. The Federal Deposit Insurance Corporation insured personal bank deposits. Big government seemed to be permanent.

Kissimmee: The Birthplace of Aviation Legislation

The *Kissimmee Valley Gazette* of July 17, 1908, carried a story of the city's ordinance prescribing the limits of flight, annual license requirements, and specifications for brakes, lights, and signal systems. When the article appeared, probably fewer than a dozen persons had flown in powered airplanes anywhere.

The *Gazette* speculated that "the ordinance will doubtless serve as a model to municipalities throughout the civilized world." And it did. Letters were received from all over the nation and the world asking for copies. It became the model for legislation in France and Germany. The War Department requested a copy for its archives.

The author of the document had not been all that serious. City Attorney P. A. Vans Agnew and Mayor T. M. Murphy had joked about it in a discussion of the future of flight. While recuperating from an injury a few weeks later, the attorney amused himself by drafting the ordinance, which he sent to the *Gazette*. Upon reading it, the mayor joked that he had been ridiculed out of town and was leaving for California, but Vans Agnew placated him by pointing out that unborn generations would benefit from the wisdom of his administration. Actually, the ordinance was never enacted by the city of Kissimmee, but it did become the model for legislation elsewhere and made Kissimmee the birthplace of aviation legislation. ➤

▲ *Women pack cigars in a Tampa cigar factory, 1930s. (Florida Historical Society)*

▼ *Apalachicola oyster shuckers, 1938. (Tampa-Hillsborough County Public Library)*

The Tourists Return

New Deal relief programs alleviated suffering and mitigated the crisis but did not restore the economy of Florida. It was probably the Second World War that accomplished that. In the meantime, many segments of the economy were improving by the mid-1930s. Tourism had never stopped, since many of those who wintered at Palm Beach were unaffected by the adversities of the depression, but the number of annual visitors to Florida dropped to less than a half-million in 1932. That had changed by 1935 when nearly two million tourists came. Building permits for hotels and residential construction dropped to less than $400,000 in 1932 but exceeded $9 million in 1936. A line of modern hotels was rising along Collins Avenue on Miami Beach, and other communities were sharing in the revival of the construction industry.

The Murphy Act

One of the most perplexing problems resulting from the collapse of the 1920s boom was the thousands of real estate parcels that had been abandoned by buyers. Local communities had begun to compromise delinquent taxes with resident owners in order to raise revenue, but what could be done about property that had simply been abandoned? The 1937 legislature resorted to an unusual remedy with the Murphy Act, which permitted the sale of tax-delinquent land for tax certificates. Far-sighted buyers thus obtained deeds to abandoned real estate at bargain prices, and the public benefited by getting it back on the tax rolls.

Pulpwood and Managed Forests

▲ *Following the harvesting of most of Florida's virgin timber, towns depending on this industry were abandoned on a large scale in the 1930s. (Pace Library—University of West Florida)*

The replanting of cutover lands by the Florida Forest Service, the Civilian Conservation Corps, and private landowners coincided with a decision of the nation's newspaper publishers to use newsprint made from pulpwood to create a new industry and return the cutover forest lands to productive use. Alfred Du Pont's St. Joe Paper Company began buying thousands of acres of west Florida land from which it planned to supply its new paper mill at Port St. Joe. The International Paper Company had already opened a pulp mill at Panama City in 1931. Other paper companies followed suit until a large portion of the state's cutover land was being replanted in pines. These new forests have since been managed according to modern conservation practices and are harvested just as any other crop, except that the growth cycle is longer.

The Citrus Industry

Florida's citrus industry had recovered from the freezes of the 1890s and had expanded across the central part of the state by the 1930s. There had also been great progress in resolving the transportation and marketing problems that had plagued the early growers. Beginning in 1909, the Florida Citrus Exchange had encouraged a common policy for the citrus industry. Local exchanges were formed to take advantage of volume buying and selling. But problems continued because many growers preferred to remain independent. Although grove acreage and the volume of production increased during the 1920s, Florida growers were still

◄ A turpentine still in Florida's panhandle, as recorded by Dorothea Lang in 1939. (Pace Library—University of West Florida)

► Preparation for the Epiphany ceremony in the Greek community of Tarpon Springs, 1934. Greeks originally came to this Gulf Coast community to dive for sponges. (Florida Historical Society)

◄ The University of Miami as it appeared during its opening in the 1930s. (Historical Association of Southern Florida)

unable to obtain satisfactory marketing and transportation arrangements. Because of their superior organization and their relationship with the railroad companies, Californians could ship fruit to the northeastern United States at more favorable rates than could Floridians. A lingering problem had been the shipment of green fruit. When one grower shipped immature fruit, all Florida citrus was damaged.

These problems still plagued the Florida Citrus Exchange in the 1930s, but the problem was more acute because citrus had become a major part of the state's agricultural production. To deal with the industry's problems, the state legislature created the citrus commission in 1935. Financed by a tax on citrus, the new agency undertook an aggressive advertising campaign and encouraged growers to protect their own interests by shipping only fruit of good quality.

Winter Vegetables

Drainage of the Everglades was a far more complex undertaking than Governor Broward's campaign slogan that "water runs downhill." Nevertheless, drainage had begun in 1906 and continued at an uneven pace over the next two decades. The Florida East Coast Railroad had encouraged the production of sugar cane and winter vegetables and had extended spurs to both Okeechobee and Belle Glade. The U.S. Department of Agriculture had established a sugar cane experiment station at Canal Point, and the state opened another at Belle Glade. Interest in the drainage project had spawned several limited booms in land sales. William J. Connors, for example, acquired about 12,000 acres of Everglades land on which he attempted to raise livestock. But the vast area was not freed from flooding problems until the national government erected a thirty-four-foot dike around Lake Okeechobee and improved the drainage canals leading from it. By that time B.G. Dahlberg had formed the company that was the predecessor of the United States Sugar Corporation to grow sugar cane in the Clewiston area.

Winter vegetables had been grown intermittently in southern Florida for many years, but growers had been hampered by marketing and drainage problems. That began to change in the 1930s, and Herman Hamilton Wedgworth had as much to do with it as any individual. In April 1930, Wedgworth became a plant pathologist at the University of Florida's Everglades Experimental Station near Belle Glade and began developing disease-resistant vegetables and fertilizers suitable to the rich but nutrient-deficient muck soil. Wedgworth soon left the University and made Wedgworth Farms the first successful producer of celery in the Everglades, although the Chase family had already earned for Sanford the appellation "Celery City" in the early 1900s. With a packing and precooling plant in Belle Glade, Wedgworth began shipping vegetables in refrigerated cars in 1934. Others joined him, and the Everglades finally became a major producer of celery, potatoes, beans, lettuce, peas, and cabbage. The lessons learned in the Everglades were applied in the mucklands north of Lake Apopka, where the Duda family and a handful of neighbors were soon producing a similar array of crops.

Wings in the Sun

Florida's fascination with the airplane began with exhibition flights at Orlando,

◄ Women made up the ranks of employees at this Plant City fruit processing plant, May 16, 1935. Note the "No Talking" warning to women who inspected the strawberries. Their children attended "strawberry schools." (Florida State Archives)

◄ The driver of this pedal taxi, or "Afro-mobile," waits for customers in a choice spot outside the Cartier jewelry store in West Palm Beach, 1939. (Library of Congress)

▲ *Reflecting the popu-*
larity of air travel,
Miami Senior High
School created a co-ed
aviation class as part of
its curriculum in the
1930s. (Historical Asso-
ciation of Southern
Florida)

The Buccaneer Route

National Airlines got its start in 1934 with a low bid of seventeen cents per mile for a government mail route from St. Petersburg to Daytona Beach. With three single-engine Ryan airplanes similar to Lindbergh's *Spirit of St. Louis*, G. T. "Ted" Baker began operations out of St. Petersburg on October 15, 1934. Lakeland and Orlando were soon added to the route after FERA provided assistance for improvements of their landing fields. Mail was flown over the central Florida route to Daytona Beach, where it was picked up by Eastern Airlines. During its first year of operations, the infant airline carried a total of 400 passengers.

That inauspicious beginning was sufficient for survival, and National successfully competed with Pan American and Eastern during the early years. Its route was extended from Daytona to Jacksonville and from St. Petersburg to Miami in 1937. A new route from Jacksonville to New Orleans was added the following year. During World War II, National moved its headquarters to Jacksonville, added new and larger aircraft, participated in the war effort, expanded its service to New York, and began billing itself as "The Buccaneer Route." During the postwar years, the airline continued to expand, competing with Eastern, Pan American, Delta (which had begun as a crop-dusting operation in 1934), and other lines. At its zenith, National provided service to much of the United States, the Caribbean islands, and Central and South America. It was amalgamated with Pan American in early 1980.

Miami, and Tampa less than a decade after the Wright brothers made their historic flight at Kitty Hawk in 1903. In 1914, Tony Jannus made history with the first regularly scheduled commercial flights in history from St. Petersburg to Tampa. About the same time Glen Curtis opened a flying school at Miami. Pensacola became the center for naval aviation in 1917. In 1918, Carl Kuhl of Orlando built an airplane before earning his wings as the state's first licensed pilot. A source of income for commercial aviators came with the Kelly Air Mail Act of 1925, which authorized contracts for specified mail routes. Pan American Airways began flying between Key West and Cuba in 1927 before moving its headquarters to Miami the following year. In 1930, Eddie Rickenbacker and Harold Pitcairn changed the name of their fledgling company to Eastern Airlines and began the first passenger service from Miami to the north.

Orlando opened a municipal airport in 1928, and Miami followed suit in early 1929. Tampa's Drew Field—originally a private landing field on the site of present-day Tampa International Airport—was leased by the city in 1928 and expanded with WPA assistance in 1934. Jacksonville had also provided flying facilities during the 1930s.

With more suitable flying days per year than most places in the nation, Florida was in a strong position when the Army Air Corps began looking for places to train its pilots as the United States started preparing for war in the late 1930s. By 1940, air bases were established at Miami, Tampa, Orlando, Jacksonville, Pensacola, and Arcadia. Many more were to follow. Military aviation became a major state industry, and its presence brought branches of aircraft supply firms to Florida. The military preparedness that continued through the 1950s kept them there. Just as the railroads had opened up the peninsula to wealthy tourists in the 1880s and the automobile had expanded Florida tourism to many more people in the 1920s, the airplane was about to do the same thing—and more—in the 1940s.

Look Ahead

The array of New Deal programs aimed at relief, recovery, and reform were winding down and international affairs were replacing them by 1940. As Floridians turned their attention from the depression that seemed to be easing to the approaching war that few wanted, they had little time to reflect on the vast changes that had been wrought by the many new agencies created in the 1930s. It would be well into the 1950s before they became aware of the vastly increased scope of governmental activity and even longer before they began to cope with it.

Chapter 12

The Second World
War, the Sunshine
State, and the
Growth Explosion
1941–1960

◄ *Urging visitors to return to Florida, this 1953 Welcome Station near Cottondale epitomized both the state's* *dependence on tourism and the declining standards of architecture. (Florida State Archives)*

▲ *On leave from nearby Camp Blanding, World War II soldiers check out the pleasures of Starke, Florida. (Florida State Archives)*

▲ *Displaying military discipline, members of the Women's Army Corps (WAC) parade through the streets of Miami. (Historical Association of Southern Florida)*

*T*he Japanese attack on Pearl Harbor on Sunday, December 7, 1941, galvanized America. A nation that had been grappling with doubt and depression for a decade was quickly changed into an industrial giant that supplied its own military forces and those of its allies scattered all over the world in a two-front war. At the same time the country put 17 million men and women in uniform—as many as 11 million at one time. The war also put the nation on the move. People traveled farther from home in greater numbers than ever before. Like their counterparts in other states, Floridians flocked to join the armed forces and home defense efforts, and went to work in factories and on farms engaged in "war production." Blackout drills were held, scrap drives were launched, war bonds and stamps were purchased, scarce commodities were rationed, and almost every family had a victory garden in the back yard. Americans were enthusiastically united in a common cause described by Martin Andersen of the *Orlando Sentinel* as "an all-out venture for victory." Women went to work in defense jobs. Both men and women took second jobs as unemployment was replaced by a severe labor shortage. It was not exceptional that the Jones Shipyard in Panama City built Liberty Ships with a work force comprised of numerous farmers from western Florida and southern Alabama, several prize fighters, one doctor of philosophy, thirteen preachers, and the entire membership of the "Original Silas Green New Orleans Show."

When men between the ages of twenty-one and thirty-six responded to the nation's first peacetime draft in history, they expected to be gone for only a year, but the Japanese altered that. Obliged to remain in service for "the duration and six months," the draftees were joined by thousands more who volunteered in the weeks following the attack on Pearl Harbor.

Two weeks after Pearl Harbor, Floridians read about Colin Kelly, Jr., the young man from Madison County who had died heroically in an air-sea battle halfway around the world. Similar stories made other young men eager to join the armed forces and those who remained at home willing to endure wartime rationing of tires, gasoline, sugar, and other scarce items. Nor did Floridians have to look far to see evidence of hostilities.

U-boats in the Gulf Stream

Most of the oil needed for defense plants on the eastern coast was transported by tankers from Gulf ports, and German submarines preyed on them in the Gulf Stream just off the Florida coast. Army Air Corps personnel first patrolled for submarines in B-18s, but the task was taken over in early 1942 by the Navy's Gulf Sea Frontier with headquarters at Miami. During the first year of the war more than two dozen tankers were sunk—three in one week near Cape Canaveral and four within sight of Miami. Some survivors from sunken vessels were rescued by people plying the same waters in pleasure boats.

Rumors of German sailors walking the streets of Miami were exacerbated by the actual landing of four German spies from a submarine near Ponte Vedra on June 17, 1942. The four Germans made their way undetected into Jacksonville, where they registered at the Mayflower and Seminole hotels before moving northward hoping to wreak havoc by bombing defense plants, electric facilities, and transportation centers. All four spies were apprehended within two weeks, tried and found guilty of sabotage, and executed. But their successful landing brought the war home to Floridians, who subsequently volunteered for home defense work in great numbers.

Florida became a huge training camp for the armed services. The six military airfields already in the state in 1940 were increased until there were forty in 1945. The Naval Air Station at Pensacola was augmented by another at Jacksonville, and Key West became a submarine base. Eglin Field was opened at Valparaiso and has since become the largest air base in the nation; Camp Blanding near Starke became a major army training station. Tourist facilities at Miami were converted into military training posts. More than 70,000 hotel rooms were used for housing military personnel, and restaurants became mess halls. Other resort cities emulated Miami. By the end of the war, nearly a quarter of all Army Air Force personnel had attended schools on Miami Beach, and thousands more from all branches of service had trained in other Florida locations. These men and thousands of family members who visited them remembered Florida in a favorable way after the war ended.

The Sunshine State

Favorable recollections of Florida's balmy climate combined with the increasing mobility and affluence of Americans to stimulate a flow of both visitors and

▲ *Part of the U.S. Navy's Mosquito Fleet, this PT boat cruises the waters around Miami during World War II. (Historical Association of Southern Florida)*

◀ Celebrities as well as the man-on-the-street signed up for service during World War II. A clean-shaven Clark Gable trains in Miami as an ordinary rank-and-file soldier. (Historical Association of Southern Florida)

▼ Enjoying the night-life of Tampa's black community, residents and visitors congregate at Watts Sanderson's Central Terrace Beer Garden in July 1942 for a little fun and social-izing. (University of South Florida Library—Special Collection)

▲ Black soldiers and friends enjoy a night out at the local USO club in Pensacola. (Pensacola Historical Society)

▶ A native of Lakeland, Frances Langford traveled with Bob Hope and the USO troop singing her way to stardom during World War II. She made frequent visits to her hometown, often bringing along her first husband, Jon Hall. After divorcing Hall, she married Ralph Evinrude, known for his outboard motor company. (Florida State Archives)

▲ Stationed at Tampa's
MacDill Air Force Base
during World War II,
members of a B-17 crew
gather in front of their
plane. (Florida Histori-
cal Society)

▼ New members of the
Women's Army Corps
stationed at Miami
Beach, 1942. (Histori-
cal Association of
Southern Florida)

permanent immigrants to the state after the war. Florida's population grew by nearly half between 1940 and 1950, and then by almost 80 percent in the next decade. By 1960 nearly five million people called Florida home. The increase of total population was decidedly uneven. Most of the growth was in the peninsula and concentrated in the cities. By 1980 most Floridians lived in the southern part of the state, and nearly three-fourths of them inhabited about a fourth of the land.

New Issues and New Institutions

In a brief period Florida had been changed from a comparatively small, rural state to a populous one that was predominantly urban. While the state's governing institutions had expanded in response to New Deal measures in the 1930s, Floridians had generally agreed with Governor Fred Cone when he deemphasized growth in the late 1930s. Although Governor Spessard Holland's administration had built nearly two thousand miles of new roads between 1941 and 1945, the war had generally overshadowed local matters. The demand for expanded public services to meet the needs of a rapidly growing population reached almost emergency proportions in the immediate postwar years. Returning servicemen using the new GI bill crowded the colleges, while the children of new immigrants swelled an already overcrowded public school system. Road construction did not keep up with growth, especially in the urban areas where suburban housing projects began spreading into the countryside. Major arterial roads became more dangerous as the increasing number of travelers more frequently encountered cattle still enjoying the freedom of the open range. The devastation of much of the state by a huge hurricane in 1947 demonstrated the need for better control of water resources.

Educating the Young

The legislature responded in 1947 to the recommendations of a committee headed by future governor LeRoy Collins and enacted the Minimum Foundation Program that still underlies the state's public education policies. It also provided for extensive expansion of the colleges, a policy that eventually led to today's system of state universities and community colleges.

Closing the Open Range

Although some counties had fenced cattle off the roads by local initiative, cattlemen had successfully resisted state legislation that would have required them to fence their pastures. As the automobile became more important for both tourists and local citizens and wrecks with cattle became more frequent, the demand for action accelerated. When Fuller Warren was elected governor in 1949 after a campaign against the open range, the legislature enacted a measure that by 1951 had removed livestock from most of Florida's roads. That legislation also expanded the role of the state road department in building and maintaining the avenues of the automobile age.

▲ *Tending the herd, Seminoles watch over their stock of cattle on the Brighton Reservation, 1950. (Florida State Archives)*

◄ Bahamian migrant laborers arrive at the Miami airport in 1943 for work in U.S. fields. The shortage of male farm workers during World War II made it necessary to import labor from neighboring countries. (Historical Association of Southern Florida)

▲ A common sight on Florida highways before a 1950 law signaled the end of the open range. Accidents caused by wandering animals reduced the ranchers' livestock and posed a danger to unsuspecting motorists. (Florida State Archives)

▶ A grandfather and his grandson ride the range on the Brighton reservation. (Florida State Archives)

▲ Replacing the hovels of the 1930s migrant camps, the Farm Security Administration provided new housing for workers at the Osceola Migratory Labor Camp in Belle Glade, 1945. (Historical Association of Southern Florida)

Managing the Flow of Water

More than forty years after Governor Broward's call for draining the Everglades, the 1947 hurricane demonstrated the need for flood control that might not only minimize the damages of too much water but that could also store the surplus for use during drought periods. While the U.S. Army Corps of Engineers began construction of a series of dams on the Apalachicola and Chattahoochee rivers to alleviate flooding in that region and provide the abundant recreation facilities of today's Lake Seminole, the legislature created the Central and South Florida Flood Control District. In cooperation with the Corps of Engineers, that agency has lessened the damages of floods and droughts in south Florida, although it has not achieved the balance of nature that existed there before man interfered.

The Park

While the flood-control project would bring great changes to the Everglades, the creation of the Everglades National Park in 1947 was both the culmination of a long campaign by several persistent conservationists and a portent of the future. The Florida Federation of Women's Clubs had begun lobbying for conservation of the Everlades almost as soon as drainage began. They persisted in their cause over the years and gradually gained other supporters. By the 1940s both Governor Holland and Governor Caldwell were in their camp. John Pennekamp of the *Miami Herald* added his considerable voice. With encouragement and financial assistance from the state legislature, the park was established and President Harry Truman dedicated it in 1947. In the years since, the Everglades National Park and Florida's other national parks have emphasized the importance of preserving the natural environment while providing recreational facilities for tourists and permanent residents.

The Profits of an Uncertain World

The shooting war was soon succeeded by the Cold War and international affairs remained unstable. Many military installations were maintained and became permanent assets to the economies of Jacksonville, Pensacola, Tampa, and many other localities. When fighting began in Korea, other bases that had been placed on standby were reopened. Thousands of military personnel continued to train and live in Florida. Government contracts and military payrolls stimulated the economy, and Floridians accepted their military neighbors. Even when the Korean conflict ended, the international tension continued and so did military preparedness. As time passed and members of the armed forces began to retire, they remembered Florida favorably. In recent decades hundreds of thousands of them have made their retirement homes in the state.

The Price of Uncertainty and Rapid Change

Like Americans everywhere, Floridians paid a price for the continued armed truce. Locked in a struggle for world domination with a nation whose ideology was antithetical to theirs, they were alarmed when Russia exploded an atom bomb in 1949. No longer did they feel secure behind the two wide oceans that had

▲ *Celebrating the end of World War II, Miami residents look forward to the return of friends and relatives. (Historical Association of Southern Florida)*

▲ Elder members of the
Seminole tribe in south
Florida lounge around
a symbol of modern
technology and give
evidence that no social
group is immune to
"progress." (Historical
Association of Southern
Florida)

▲ Displaying their
hospitality, Governor
and Mrs. LeRoy
Collins welcome a dele-
gation of Seminoles
to the Governor's
Mansion, 1956. (Flor-
ida State Archives)

▶ This clapboard hous-
ing unit for black
migrant workers in
Pahokee was facetiously
referred to by its occu-
pants as the "Pahokee
Hotel," 1941. (Library of
Congress)

▲ *Photographer John Collier captures the essence of the small rural town of Baker, Florida, in 1942. (Pace Library—University of West Florida)*

▲ *Investigating crime in the United States, Senator Estes Kefauver of Tennessee (left) and Senator Lester Hunt of Wyoming (center) discuss suspected gambling syndicates in south Florida with Dan Sullivan (right), investigator for the Miami Crime Commission, 1950. (Historical Association of Southern Florida)*

traditionally protected them. Their world seemed to be shrinking as a result of rapid transportation, instant communications, and intercontinental weaponry. At the same time the role of government was becoming more obtrusive. After years of debate, the legislature authorized a state sales tax in 1949 to pay for the services its citizens were coming to expect. While that measure was received with mixed feelings, the national government's increasing attention to long-standing racial arrangements caused outright alarm. Years of growing governmental activity, threats to social customs, and what seemed to be a perpetual international threat left Floridians apprehensive about the future and receptive to purveyors of simple solutions.

McCarthyism and "Red" Pepper

Wisconsin Senator Joseph McCarthy's rantings about Communists in the national government appealed to Americans fearful of Russian armament from without and "creeping communism" from within. A genuine "Red scare" swept the nation and engulfed Florida's senatorial election of 1950. A U.S. senator since 1936, Claude Pepper had portrayed himself as a staunch New Dealer and a devout liberal at a time when liberalism was losing popularity. He had also visited Russia in 1947 on one of his many overseas junkets. Miamian George Smathers seized the opportunity to question Pepper's loyalty and suggested that the incumbent senator was a defender of Joseph Stalin and his loathsome policies. Perhaps more damning, Smathers also pointed out that Pepper had approved a Fair Employment Practices Commission aimed at improving the lot of blacks seeking work. Well-intended efforts to increase the number of black voters so that they could support Pepper in 1950 caused a backlash as more white voters went to the polls. In an election that unfortunately linked the issues of communism and civil rights for blacks, George Smathers easily defeated Pepper and served three terms in the U.S. Senate. Pepper moved to Miami Beach and was elected to a seat in the House of Representatives, a position he held for over twenty-five years.

Television and Coonskin Caps

In both Miami and Tampa, official corruption lubricated by payoffs from gambling organizations had become sources of embarrassment by midcentury. Gambling casinos operated by gangsters and wide-open bookmaking became the target of a Miami citizens' committee in 1949. Led by the *Miami Herald* and the *Miami News*, the committee determined to clean up the town. For months the newspapers and radio stations featured stories about gambling operations and named those involved. In Tampa, bolita had begun as a relatively harmless lottery imported with the Cuban cigar makers, but it had become big business by the late 1940s. Deprived of revenues by the repeal of Prohibition in the 1930s and the crackdown on prostitution in the early 1940s, gamblers had taken over and expanded the bolita games. Racketeering and political corruption were besmirching the reputation of Tampa throughout the country.

Old-fashioned enough to realize the advantage of campaigning for his rural constituency in a coonskin cap and modern enough to recognize the value of the new television medium, Tennessee Senator Estes Kefauver brought his Senate

▲ Representatives of Walt Disney Productions drink a glass of Donald Duck orange juice at the Lake Wales Citrus Canners Cooperative, November 1951. Was this the drink that launched a billion tourists? (Tampa-Hillsborough County Public Library)

◀ Miami Beach's famous hotel row in November 1957. (Historical Association of Southern Florida)

▶ *With news of the war to keep them informed, air conditioning to soothe their spirits, and films to entertain them, 1942 moviegoers depended on the Tampa Theatre for information and recreation. (Florida Historical Society)*

▲ *Unable to break into the world of white-collar industry, many Southern blacks occupied the role of laborers. These Floridians work in the commercial fishing business sorting shrimp for marketing. (Tampa-Hillsborough County Public Library)*

▲ *A teacher conducts class at the Big Cypress reservation day school for Seminole Indian children, 1940. (Historical Association of Southern Florida)*

◀ *In 1947, green turtles destined for northern soup pots line the terminals of the Barton H. Smith Company in Tampa. (Florida Historical Society)*

◀ *Black employees sort gladiolas for shipping at the ACW Bulb Company in Fort Myers, 1945. At one time, Lee County was recognized as having the world's largest gladiola industry. (Tampa-Hillsborough County Public Library)*

▲ *Showing the progress and growth of modern technology, Tallahassee's Southeastern Telephone Company switchboard operators handle the influx of calls from city customers, 1949. (Florida State Archives)*

▶ *Belle Glade farm laborers work in a celery field, 1947. (Florida State Archives)*

▲ *A young boy fills his wagon with Spanish moss from a Leesburg moss yard in 1946. (Florida State Archives)*

crime commission to Florida and exposed the gambling syndicates of Miami and Tampa to a national viewing audience. In the process Governor Fuller Warren was shown to have accepted illegal campaign contributions from a known gambler, the sheriffs of Dade and Hillsborough counties were removed from office, and other public officials were exposed. In the long run, the Kefauver exposures helped the local reformers immeasurably in cleaning up their cities, but they also accentuated the feeling among Floridians that they were being included in a world that they had once been better able to hold at arm's length.

Increasing Racial Tensions

Mounting racial tensions erupted into violence before excitement over the Smathers-Pepper campaign and the Kefauver investigation had subsided. Harry T. Moore, secretary of the National Association for the Advancement of Colored People (NAACP) and founder of the Progressive Voters' League, had launched a drive to register black voters in the late 1940s, a movement that received considerable attention in the 1950 election. At about the same time, national attention was drawn to the so-called Groveland riots and Lake County Sheriff Willis McCall's sensational handling of four young black men accused of raping a white woman. Moore's insistence that McCall be called to account for his actions raised the ire of some Floridians. The Reverend Theodore Gibson, head of the Miami chapter of the NAACP, also attracted attention when he refused to turn over his membership rolls to the FBI. The bombing of Carver Village, a black housing project in Miami, several other bombings and cross burnings, and the killing of Harry Moore and his wife by a bomb that exploded under their bedroom on Christmas 1951 brought on a national outcry. While die-hard segregationists remained unmoved, moderate Floridians were generally appalled. Some communities established biracial committees to seek solutions to their problems.

The Leavening Hand of Governor LeRoy Collins

By the early 1950s, blacks were demanding readmission to the mainstream of society on a variety of fronts. While it continued to push for voter registration and equal employment opportunities, the NAACP had been challenging segregation of public facilities for more than a generation. By the late 1940s, it was winning Supreme Court decisions in favor of integrated professional and graduate schools. Despite such developments, however, Floridians were shocked by the 1954 decision in *Brown v. Board of Education*, which called for an end to segregated public schools.

Emphasizing his determination to do everything legally possible to preserve Florida's social arrangements, Governor LeRoy Collins called on his fellow Floridians to obey the law of the land and later declared that segregation was morally wrong. In the face of overwhelming opposition from the white public and a legislature determined to defy the court decision, Collins patiently called for moderation. Although he paid a heavy political price for taking the high road in the school desegregation crisis, Governor Collins guided his state through the tense years without the confrontations and ugliness that occurred in some Southern states. It would still be many years before segregation was removed, but by the late 1960s progress was being made.

▲ *Preparing for one of their infamous night meetings, members of the Ku Klux Klan gather in Tallahassee, 1956. (Florida State Archives)*

◄ *A well-stocked bar and "jook joint" becomes a gathering place for migrant laborers in south central Florida, 1941. (Library of Congress)*

◄ *Carrying on a tradition that began around the turn of the century, this unidentified black women's club poses for a portrait before the start of their meeting. (Florida State Archives)*

▲ *One of Key West's most famous residents, author Ernest Hemingway was attracted to the easy lifestyle of this island colony. (Historical Association of Southern Florida)*

Promoting Economic Development

During the Collins administration the legislature established the Florida Development Commission to centralize all promotional work and the International Trade Department to stimulate foreign trade and travel. Collins also made many appearances throughout the country emphasizing the attractions of the state for tourism, immigration, and industrial relocation. While such initiatives would be continued and expanded by subsequent administrations and would eventually prove fruitful, Florida's economy was immediately stimulated more by actions from without rather than from within the state. The U.S. Missile Test Center opened at Cape Canaveral in 1950 and soon made Brevard County the fastest-growing area of the state. It also attracted Martin Marietta and dozens of smaller space- and defense-related industries to the area. Creation of the National Aeronautics and Space Administration (NASA) in 1958 to explore space operations of a scientific nature added another dimension to the central Florida growth explosion. The 1960 population of Brevard County was nearly four times that of 1950, and the population would double again by 1970. Cattle ranches and citrus groves began to feel the pressure of expanding suburbs all around Orlando and the smaller coastal cities.

Carrying the Past into the Future

While addressing new opportunities, Floridians were having to make decisions about their traditional values by the late 1950s. The stimulus of the new Space Center and an aggressive development policy on the part of state government was generating a new wave of economic growth. That growth was creating an interdependence between state and national policies that spilled over into social and political matters. The events of the post–World War II era had collectively contributed to a challenge of many long-held beliefs, and technological advances were making the world seem smaller while time seemed to move faster. Floridians were obliged to adjust to an age of uncertainty in international affairs, the extension of the democratic promise to citizens from whom it had been denied, a society in which outside forces were influencing their lives to a greater degree than ever before, and an era of expansion that would eventually dwarf the boom of the 1920s.

▶ *The Joie Chitwood Auto Daredevils perform for fans at the 1951 Florida State Fair. (Tampa-Hillsborough County Public Library)*

▶ An employee of Shepard's Grist Mill located in Quincy bags corn meal for distribution, 1956. (Florida State Archives)

▲ The Florida Chip Steak booth was a popular spot at the 1956 Florida State Fair. (Tampa-Hillsborough County Public Library)

▶ Recognizable from their dress, this Mennonite couple observe the planting of crops on a farm located in the vicinity of Sarasota, 1941. (Library of Congress)

▲ In the 1950s, two Ocala homes were swallowed by the formation of a sinkhole. Many of the state's lakes were once sinkholes. (Florida State Archives)

Chapter 13

The Space Age,
the New Tourism,
and Another
Latin American
Connection
1961–1980

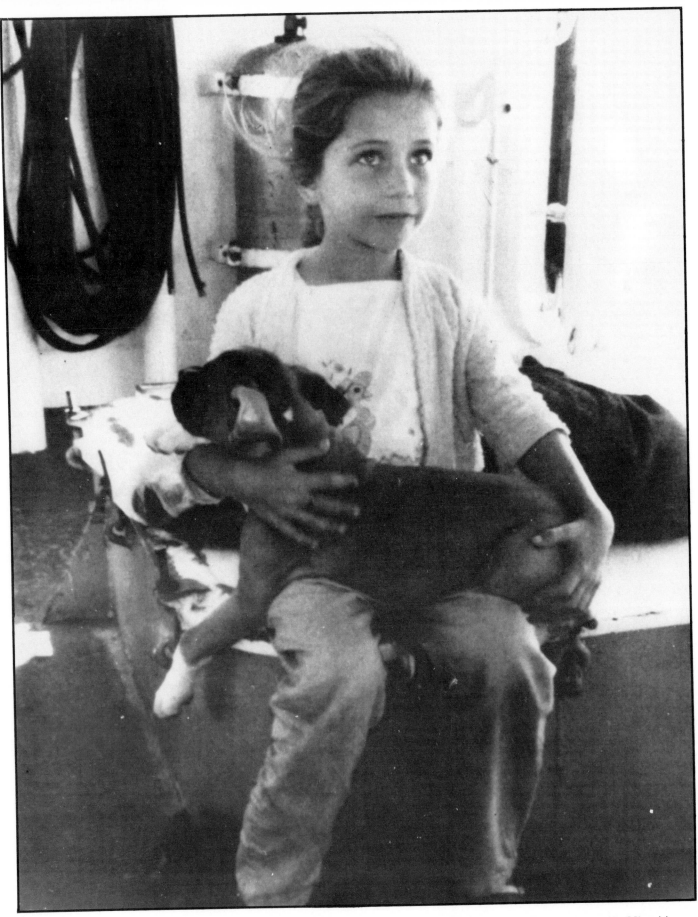

◀ *Florida's economy depends heavily on the millions of tourists who visit the state each year. Theme parks, such as Adventure Island in Tampa, provide attractive destinations for visitors, employment for residents, and substance to the legend of Florida as "The Golden Playland." (University of South Florida—Florida Collection)*

▲ *The Cuban revolution caused many Cubans to flee to the United States in the early 1960s. Leaving behind their families and worldly possessions, thousands of refugees came to Miami in search of a new home. This young Cuban arrives with her most precious possession. (Historical Association of Southern Florida)*

$\mathcal{W}$hen he announced in 1961 that NASA was launching a program to land a man on the moon, President John F. Kennedy stimulated another acceleration in the growth of central Florida and focused national attention on the entire state for years. The project was soon employing 25,000 people, and dozens of supporting firms were adding greatly to that number. The population of central Florida mushroomed as people moved there to support the space program; tourists by the thousands came to watch the spectacular launches while Walter Cronkite and his colleagues provided live television coverage for the rest of the nation.

A Man on the Moon

The hordes of new immigrants strained the capacities of local governments to provide schools, roads, and other public accommodations. Suburbs sprawled around every town within commuting distance of Cape Canaveral. By 1968 an average of 57,000 visitors were touring the Kennedy Space Center each day. The zenith was reached in 1969 when millions of television viewers watched Walter Cronkite gasp his admiring approval of the first man to walk on the moon.

The space program fluctuated from the early 1970s until the disastrous explosion of the shuttle *Challenger* in early 1986 slowed it to a near halt. But space research and travel has gradually recovered, and Spaceport USA remains one of the major tourist attractions in central Florida.

The New Cuban Immigration

Since the sixteenth century, when Spanish Florida was controlled through Cuba, the island nation and the southern Florida communities had maintained close contact in a variety of ways. During the twentieth century, Miami had become the home of exiled Cuban presidents driven from power by the frequent revolutions and of exiles awaiting the next change of government. Fidel Castro's overthrow of Fulgencio Batista in early 1959 was at first regarded as yet another in a long line of revolutionary changes. A large number of Cubans boarded planes from Miami and headed for the Cuban homeland, hailing Castro as a liberating hero. But it was not long before some of them were heading back. Revelations of the firing squad executions of hundreds of his political opponents and his plans for a Communist-style government horrified and distressed many of his countrymen. By the summer of 1960, six planes a day were carrying a steady stream of expatriate Cubans from the island. A sympathetic Miami populace welcomed the refugees, who at first expected to return home as soon as the political situation changed. But it did not change. The exile became permanent, the numbers of refugees increased, and Miami was changed forever.

Failed Filibustering and Missiles Ninety Miles Away

To accelerate the fall of Castro, a brigade of Cuban freedom fighters, aided by the CIA, trained in the Everglades and launched an invasion of Cuba in April 1961. The Bay of Pigs landing was a disaster after the United States called off its promised air support. Newly elected President John F. Kennedy had interceded to halt what he believed was an erroneous foreign policy, but the exiled Cubans in Miami felt that he had let them down. The other side of that policy emerged in the fall of 1962 when it was learned that Russians were building missile launch pads in Cuba. When President Kennedy ordered a blockade of the island in October 1962, a crisis atmosphere spread over the nation and army units moved into Dade County. After a few tense days, Nikita Khrushchev agreed to remove the missiles. A relieved American ambassador said that "we were eyeball to eyeball and the other side blinked," but everyone was relieved that the confrontation ended peacefully.

Ethnic-styled Urban Renewal

A firmly entrenched Fidel Castro continued his repressive policies while more of his countrymen came to Florida. Their hopes of returning to Cuba diminished as the years passed. Castro agreed to two "freedom flights" per day beginning in 1965 and lasting until 1973. By the late 1970s, more than 600,000 Cubans had emigrated to the United States. While many moved on to other parts of Florida and the nation, the vast majority have remained in Miami.

A proud, industrious, and generally well-educated people, the Cubans quickly went to work and began overcoming the losses they had suffered when they left their homeland. In doing so, they have revitalized the decaying inner city of Miami, which has become a thriving population center with a distinctly Latin flavor. In the stores and restaurants and along the streets Spanish is the dominant language. Much of the rest of the city has become bilingual. Many of the younger

▲ *Facing an uncertain future, the strain of leaving their homeland is reflected in the face of these Cuban refugees. (Historical Association of Southern Florida)*

Cubans have become citizens and have begun to vote in large numbers. Both Cubans and Puerto Ricans have been elected to local and state offices in recent years. The intense anticommunism of the Cubans has made them quite conservative politically, a factor destined to alter the traditionally liberal voting pattern of Miami and Dade County. The Cuban population's special attitudes about Castro and communism have also made Miami one of the few local governments in the United States with its own foreign policy. Local politicians exercise great care in addressing local issues, which can often become linked to sensitive foreign policies.

The Tourism Revolution

After the mammoth land acquisitions that the government had made in connection with the space program and such huge private transactions as Martin Marietta's purchase of 7,300 acres in 1956, central Floridians assumed another defense firm was behind the rumored purchase of large tracts in southwest Orange County in 1965. Most were quite surprised when Walt Disney flew into Orlando in November of that year and revealed plans for a development that would permanently alter life in the Orlando area and the Florida tourist industry forever. Armed with fee-simple deeds to 27,000 acres of raw land and a state law granting him governmental powers over it, Disney told an admiring crowd that he was launching construction on phase one of a multistaged development. The initial project was construction of a comprehensive vacation resort, including hotels, restaurants, shopping centers, and a "Magic Kingdom" theme park similar to Disneyland in California but "bigger and better." Phase two was an Environmental Prototype Community of Tomorrow (EPCOT) to be built later.

Hailed as the largest nongovernmental construction project in the nation, the first phase employed more than 4,000 people for its construction. Scheduled to open in 1971, the resort was already entertaining 85,000 visitors a month by 1969 with its Disney World Preview Center featuring motion pictures and models. During its first two years, Disney World had more than 20 million paying visitors, had gross receipts of $3.2 billion, and employed 13,000 people with an annual payroll of $365 million. It has subsequently employed more than 18,000 people at one time and has frequently entertained more than one million paying visitors a month.

Revelation of the Disney project was cataclysmic to central Florida. Land values in Osceola, Orange, and Seminole counties soared. Multimillion dollar transactions became commonplace as investors purchased sites that seemed suitable for hotels, service stations, restaurants, and other facilities ancillary to the coming attraction. Most Floridians applauded Walt Disney and enjoyed the boom, but there were some dissenters. Retirees did not enjoy the escalation of property values and corresponding increases in their taxes, and travelers were often vexed by the hours-long traffic jams on the highways that the Disney project caused and which the firm has consistently refused to help alleviate. A few observers resent—and fear—the anomaly of a private corporation being endowed with the same governing powers as a city or county and wish that the highly prosperous Disney World would become a better neighbor and share some of the burdens

◀ Palm trees, sandy beaches, theme parks, and year-round activities have made Florida the mecca for vacationers throughout the world. (University of South Florida— Florida Collection)

▲ Florida's perpetual sunshine has attracted retirees from across the nation for a daily diet of golf, fishing, and sunbathing. (University of South Florida— Florida Collection)

caused by the phenomenal growth it stimulated.

Competitors in the tourism industry feared that the comprehensive Disney facility would dwarf everything else. Hotel owners at Miami Beach and elsewhere expressed special concern that Disney World would short-circuit visitors. The majority discounted such apprehensions and speculated that Disney World would attract more visitors than ever before and that the spin-off would benefit the entire tourism industry.

Other Theme Park Attractions

Whether doubters were correct is unclear. The growth of central Florida does seem to have detracted from the south Florida hotels, but Busch Gardens and numerous facilities have enjoyed their share of the market. Even historic St. Augustine has been filled with capacity crowds in recent years. Sea World, a $20 million facility that opened in 1973, has entertained as many as 20,000 visitors a day in peak season. Spaceport USA and Cypress Gardens seem also to benefit from their proximity to the huge theme park. More recently, MGM and Universal Studios are drawing visitors to central Florida.

EPCOT

The promised Environmental Prototype Community of Tomorrow, somewhat modified from its original conception, opened in 1982 and set off another wave of enthusiasm. Despite some mixed feelings about the impact of the imaginative fantasy land, Floridians seem to have welcomed the attraction and its residual benefits, despite some adverse side effects. There is a clear correlation between the Disney interests and the fact that Florida is entertaining about 40 million visitors each year.

From Natural Attractions to Theme Parks

Tourists originally came to Florida for the climate and the natural recreation offered by the forests, lakes and rivers, and the ocean. Silver Springs was an early adaptation of a natural phenomenon that in time took on manmade improvements. Cypress Gardens was a manmade adaptation on a natural theme. Busch Gardens, opened at Tampa in 1959, was among the first of the attractions based on an artificial theme, but many more were soon to follow. It was perhaps inevitable that that should happen since the state's natural environment has been shrinking rapidly in the face of tremendous population growth. However they may be viewed, the theme parks—and especially Disney World—have made tourism by far the largest industry in a state whose overall economy has mushroomed in recent years.

Social and Political Adjustments

During the 1960s Floridians continued to deal with social and political change. The civil rights movement expanded to include demands for equal access to public accommodations, and sit-ins and bus boycotts became common. Neither Farris Bryant nor Haydon Burns, who succeeded LeRoy Collins as chief executive, was

◄ Protesting the arrests of twenty-three classmates participating in a sit-in, 250 Florida A&M students demonstrate through the streets of Tallahassee. Police officers broke up the march by using tear gas to disperse the crowds. (Florida State Archives)

▼ Florida A&M's famous football coach Jake Gaither leads his team in a pregame prayer. He urged his players to be "agile, hostile, and mobile." (Florida State Archives)

▼ "Rapid" Robert Hays, a senior at Florida A&M and a native of Jacksonville, weighs in at the Tallahassee airport on his way to the Olympic trials in Los Angeles. Called the world's fastest man in the 100-yard dash—he held a 9.1-second record—Hays brought home a gold medal in the 1964 Tokyo Olympics. (Florida State Archives)

▲ *Waging war against Florida's rigid color line, blacks kneel for prayer under the watchful eyes of the Leon County sheriff patrol. (Florida State Archives)*

▲ *Staging a sit-in at a Tallahassee Woolworth lunch counter, March 15, 1960. Standing in the background are police officer Joe Gregory and City Manager Arva Hopkins. (Florida State Archives)*

as successful as Collins in dealing with the issue, but except for disturbances at St. Augustine and Liberty City and a lesser one at Jacksonville, confrontations were more verbal and legal than violent. Blacks slowly achieved their goals and legal segregation was ended. Problems of equal opportunity in employment, adequate housing, and educational advancement proved more difficult, but they are finally being addressed.

One-Man, One-Vote and the Return of the Republican Party

The preponderance of population growth in urban areas and in the lower peninsula—about one-third of all Floridians live in Palm Beach, Broward, and Dade counties—had created a serious imbalance in legislative representation in state government. Noting in 1955 that about one-fourth of the population could elect a majority of both houses of the legislature, Dade County residents insisted on change. Legislators from the sparsely populated northern Florida counties were reluctant to vote themselves out of office, however, and an impasse was reached by the early 1960s. A few modest changes by the legislature were adjudged inadequate, and the federal courts intervened in 1966. Reapportionment of the legislature on an equal population basis was ordered. The change immediately enhanced the political power of the urban areas and increased the number of Republicans in the legislature. The change coincided with the surprise election of Claude Kirk, who became Florida's first Republican governor since the end of Reconstruction in 1877.

Challenging the One-Party System

The reapportionment did not bring the abrupt changes many had anticipated, but the legislature was immediately more representative of Florida in the last half of the twentieth century and has addressed statewide issues with increasing responsibility since the change. With an entirely Democratic cabinet and a majority of Democrats in the legislature, Governor Kirk had difficulty in carrying out a consistent program, but his enthusiastic and peripatetic style attracted much national attention to the state at the same time he forced Floridians to look at some of the problems facing them. Reapportionment and the election of a Republican governor did not bring about a two-party system, but it left an identifiable minority that has been able to open up debate on important matters.

In Search of Balance: Economic Growth and Environmental Stress

The new constitution of 1968 empowered Florida governors to succeed themselves for the first time since 1885. Elected in 1970, Reuben Askew was the first to serve two full terms. Between 1971 and 1979, he followed the standard earlier set by LeRoy Collins in addressing issues according to what he deemed the public interest. In doing so, he frequently took the unpopular side of controversial questions. He won some battles and lost some, but he earned the respect of most for his courageous leadership. While he made important gains in race relations and in demonstrating that Floridians were willing to approve important changes in tax laws if adequately informed about them, Askew probably did most in continuing to promote economic development while increasing the state's responsibility for environmental quality. The election of Robert D. "Bob" Graham to succeed Askew in 1979 assured the continuation of progressive executive leadership into the critical 1980s.

Tourism had long since become a year-round industry by the 1970s, but it often fluctuated according to the health of the national economy. Both governmental and private leaders recognized the need for more stable industrial employment to even out the ups and downs of tourism. Efforts to attract new industries and to find new markets were expanded. Askew himself headed several trade missions to promote Florida exports and perhaps to attract investors and visitors. Visionary leaders promoted the idea of the state university system working with industry to encourage development, as the University of Central Florida is currently doing in conjunction with Orange County in their jointly managed Research Park.

At the same time, Florida government began accepting responsibility for the state's natural resources. Laws were enacted to control pollution and to require long-range planning for affordable development. A fund was created with which the state might purchase environmentally sensitive lands. A department of natural resources was empowered to review development and evaluate its impact on the environment. The Water Resources Act of the late 1970s divided the state into six water management districts with a view to managing what many regard as a finite water supply in the face of a burgeoning demand for it.

As Florida's population approached 10 million in the late 1970s, it was becoming increasingly clear that while growth was essential for the economic health of a rapidly growing population, the land on which the people lived was of inestimable value and had to be respected if it were to sustain a quality of life that would continue to be attractive to prospective residents and to those who possessed the power to locate their companies in the state.

◀ *Susan Deen of Bunnell, a seventeen-year-old senior, was crowned Florida's 1962 Potato Queen by Commissioner of Agriculture Doyle E. Connor during festivities held in the town of Hastings. (Florida State Archives)*

Chapter 14

*Florida in the
1980s and 1990s*

◀ A statewide network
of modern highways
connects population
centers from Pensacola
to Key West. This is an
aerial view of Interstate
275 snaking through St.
Petersburg. (Photo
courtesy Hampton
Dunn)

▲ Solving transporta-
tion problems caused by
rapid growth is a chal-
lenge Florida will face
into the next century.
Some have proposed the
use of monorail
systems to alleviate
road traffic, noise, and
pollution. Here, an elec-
tric train passes
through Walt Disney
World's Contemporary
Resort-Hotel in
Orlando. (Copyright
Walt Disney Produc-
tions; photo courtesy
Hampton Dunn)

A Florida promoter in the 1920s exulted that Florida was about to become three huge metropolitan areas. He envisioned a city sprawling from Palm Beach to Miami, another from Daytona Beach to Tampa, and a third along the Gulf Coast from Panama City to Pensacola. He was right, but his timing was wrong. The boom of the 1920s ended before that happened, but his prediction is becoming reality in the late twentieth century. More than 3 million people live along the lower east coast, where cities abut each other for a hundred miles. Development is rapidly filling the remaining usable space along Interstate 4 between Daytona and Tampa, and the Tampa Bay area is a teeming metropolis. Urbanization extends southward from there for miles, and Ft. Myers is the fastest-growing city in the state. The stretch of beach between Panama City and Pensacola is fast disappearing in the face of development. With nearly 13 million inhabitants in 1990, Florida is the fourth largest state in the nation and is still growing at a rate of more than 200,000 people every year. At least 80 percent of the population lives on less than 20 percent of the land.

The Critical Mass

Florida's enormous growth during the past forty years, coinciding with the age of the automobile and the airplane, is more accurately described as suburbanization rather than urbanization. Suburban housing projects filled up as fast as they were completed, and people commuted to work, school, and play. A system of limited-access highways and toll roads and a steadily expanding air transportation service made it easy to move in and out of the state and between the population centers. But the transportation system has not progressed at an even pace. With excellent terminal facilities such as those at Tampa, Miami, and Orlando, Floridians can move by air with ease to destinations all over North America and to many foreign destinations; once on the ground, it's a different story. Arterial highways are becoming clogged with traffic in many areas, and the streets of the cities are at times nearly impassable. The widespread suburbs make it difficult to develop suitable mass transportation, and billions of dollars worth of highway and road work are needed merely to keep up with needs. Transportation emerged as a major concern of the 1980s and will remain so into the next century.

The Golden Years

While persons of all ages come to Florida for many reasons, a large proportion of them are retirees. St. Petersburg has long been famous for its green park benches and senior citizens, but it is not unique. Nor is it only military personnel returning to the Florida they remember from their active-duty days. Retirees from all walks of life and from all income levels have made their homes in Florida. They live in suburban housing, in adult communities designed especially for them, in condominiums, and in high-rise retirement homes. But wherever they reside, they have special needs—health care and a stable tax system, for example—which are sometimes at odds with the requirements of other groups. The retirees are politically active and able to see that their voices are heard.

Public Services of Every Kind

Other Floridians have growing families. They require schools and transportation routes and jobs for themselves and their children. An expanding public school and college system is essential to them—and to many of their employers. The increasing concentration of population in smaller spaces seems to increase the number of crimes as well as the number of displaced persons who require assistance from public facilities. The judicial system, the police force, the detention facilities to deal with crime, and the welfare services to assist the unfortunate are also expensive.

Paying for Growth

When Florida had fewer than a million inhabitants and millions of acres of open land, the people prohibited a personal income tax by constitutional amendment, hoping thereby to attract more wealthy immigrants. The strategy worked. As public services expanded, the state permitted local governments to pay their way with property levies while relying on user taxes for its income until a sales tax became necessary in 1949. That tax has been increased from time to time, but it does not grow in proportion to the expanded demand for services. The gap between the demand for public facilities and the supply of funds for them is a formidable one that must eventually be addressed.

◄ With its heavily serv-
ice-oriented economy,
Florida remains
strongly dependent on
tourism. (Copyright
Walt Disney Produc-
tions; photo courtesy
Hampton Dunn)

◄ The Florida beach
where man left Earth to
walk on the moon has
become a unique tourist
attraction, visited by
thousands each week.
But the future of the
space program will
directly impact the
state's economic well-
being. (Florida Dept. of
Commerce)

▲ *In the late 1970s, another group of refugees flocked to the shores of Miami. Known as the Haitian boat people, thousands of Haitians fled their country to escape political and social repression, often arriving in small, unsafe boats such as this one. (Historical Association of Southern Florida)*

▲*On May 2, 1980, newly released refugees flee Mariel, Cuba, as Fidel Castro relaxes his long-standing closed-door policy. (Historical Association of Southern Florida)*

A State in an International World

With about 80 percent of its employment in service-related jobs, Florida remains heavily dependent on tourism, but even that industry is changing. While Canadians have wintered in Florida for many years, a growing number of Europeans and Latin Americans are also vacationing in the state. One is almost as likely to hear tourists speaking Spanish or Portuguese as English, and European languages are no longer exceptional.

Financial and industrial corporations have expanded greatly in scope, and many of them are multinational. Only twenty-five years ago, branch banking was forbidden in Florida. Although holding companies were getting around that prohibition for some time, during the 1980s Florida banking was revolutionized. Acquisitions have become commonplace, and regional mergers are creating financial institutions with enormous financial capabilities. With its large Latin population and its proximity to Caribbean and Latin American nations, Miami's banks have become international as people from those often volatile republics prefer the security of U.S. financial institutions. Foreigners from the world over have invested heavily in Florida real estate, agriculture, and even industrial firms.

Special Link with Latin America

As governor, Bob Graham traveled all over the world to promote trade, but he paid special attention to Latin America. The thousands of Haitian and Cuban émigrés flocking to south Florida were a national problem, but their physical presence made them especially Florida's. Graham explored ways the state and nation could work with Caribbean nations to improve the lot of their citizens. Some progress has been made, and the door between Florida and her Latin American neighbors is opened wider than ever before. One measure of that change is the tripling of Florida's international trade during the past decade. The value of Florida's foreign trade in 1985 was over $20 billion, and more than half of it was with Latin America. The Martinez administration has continued these policies but has concentrated its attention more on domestic matters.

While Floridians ponder the questions of how to pay for the growth that has already taken place and how to balance that of the future with the limitations of the natural environment, they must do so in an increasingly international atmosphere. Even the state school system has realized that with its belated emphasis on the study of foreign languages. As we approach the end of the century, it seems that Florida will be compelled to address its internal problems caused by the state's phenomenal growth. Those services usually referred to as infrastructure will require more attention than they have received in recent years.

Epilogue

*E*ncompassing the oldest continuous European settlement on the North American continent, Florida is sometimes viewed as a very old state among its forty-nine neighbors. But with a population derived overwhelmingly from immigration, most of it in the past forty years, the state is also very new. Caught up for centuries in the rivalries of European nations for position in the New World, Florida remained largely unpopulated during the long periods of Spanish and English occupation. Only a handful of Spanish citizens remained after the territory was acquired by the United States in the early nineteenth century. Except for St. Augustine and some historic names, the very significant Latin influence in Florida history derives from its interaction with Cuba in the years since 1821.

Florida did not evolve gradually from its sixteenth-century beginnings but is rather an eclectic transplant in the twentieth century. David Halberstam has characterized the state as a giant suburb without the ameliorating influences of a central city. Perhaps that is true and Florida is still becoming.

Florida was for many decades as much a vacation land for inhabitants of other states as it was home for its permanent residents. It also included large expanses of undeveloped land that were gradually acquired by absentee owners. As the permanent population grew and the volume of tourism increased, those absentee owners took advantage of the opportunities to profit from their real estate holdings. Florida real estate was sought by larger and larger developers, and suburban housing and shopping centers were superceded by huge planned unit developments, industrial parks, and high-rise office complexes.

First concentrated around the larger cities, these developments are spreading outward and urban areas are beginning to interlock. Such rampant growth has created problems that extend beyond the scope of local governments, and the state has begun to assume some responsibility for the solutions.

What Florida ultimately becomes will depend upon the continued cooperation among the permanent population speaking through its government, developers from within and without the state, and the tourism industry in finding a balance that will preserve the natural endowments that have made Florida so attractive in the twentieth century. That is the challenge—and the promise—as the century approaches its final decade. What Florida will be like in the next millennium depends on what its present inhabitants want to make it. ➤

B i b l i o g r a p h y

Research for *Florida Portrait* was conducted in primary sources—including personal manuscript collections, diaries, public documents, and newspapers—in the Library of Congress and the National Archives in Washington, D.C., the P. K. Yonge Library of Florida History, University of Florida, Gainesville; the Southern Historical Collection, University of North Carolina, Chapel Hill; and the Florida State Archives, Tallahassee, Florida. Valuable secondary sources on Florida were also found in the *Florida Historical Quarterly* and *Florida Trend* magazine. The following bibliography lists selected books on the state's history available in Florida libraries.

Akerman, Joe A., Jr. *Florida Cowman*. Kissimmee: Florida Cattlemen's Association, 1976.

Barbour, George M. *Florida for Tourists*. Gainesville: University of Florida Press, 1964.

Barrientos, Bartolome. *Pedro Menéndez de Avilés* (1567). Translated by Anthony Kerrigan. Gainesville: University of Florida Press, 1956.

Blake, Nelson M. *Land into Water—Water into Land*. Tallahassee: University Presses of Florida, 1980.

Brinton, Daniel B. *A Guide Book to Florida*. Philadelphia: Inquirer Printing House, 1869.

Buker, George E. *Swamp Sailors*. Gainesville: University Presses of Florida, 1975.

Bullen, Adelaide K. *Florida Indians of Past and Present*. New York and London: Kendall Books, 1974.

Burnett, Gene. *Florida's Past*. Two volumes. Sarasota: Pineapple Press, 1986 and 1988.

Carter, Clarence Edwin, compiler. *The Territorial Papers of the United States*. Vols. XXII–XXVI. Washington, D.C.: Government Printing Office, 1960.

Cohen, M. M. *Notices of Florida and the Campaigns*. Facsimile reproduction of the 1836 edition. Gainesville: University of Florida Press, 1964.

Corse, Carita Doggett. *Florida, a Guide to the Southernmost State*. Compiled and written by the Federal Writers' Projects of the Works Progress Administration for the State of Florida. New York: Oxford University Press, 1939.

Curl, Donald W. *Palm Beach County, an Illustrated History*. Brightwaters, New York: Windsor Publishing, 1986.

Davis, William Watson. *Civil War and Reconstruction in Florida*. Gainesville: University of Florida Press, 1964.

Doherty, Herbert J. *Richard Keith Call, Southern Unionist*. Gainesville: University of Florida Press, 1967.

Fisher, Jane. *Fabulous Hoosier*. Chicago: Harry Coleman and Co., 1953.

Flynt, J. Wayne. *Cracker Messiah: Governor Sidney J. Catts of Florida*. Baton Rouge: Louisiana State University Press, 1977.

Fox, Charles Donald. *The Truth about Florida*. New York: Charles Renard Corp., 1925.

Fuller, Walter P. *St. Petersburg and Its People*. St. Petersburg: Great Outdoors Publishing Co., 1972.

———. *This Was Florida's Boom*. St. Petersburg: Times Publishing Co., 1954.

Gannon, Michael V. *The Cross in the Sand*. Gainesville: University of Florida Press, 1967.

Griffin, John W. *The Florida Indian and His Neighbors*. Winter Park, Florida: Rollins College, 1949.

Hawkes, J. M. *The Florida Gazetteer*. New Orleans: 1871.

Hopkins, James T. *Fifty Years of Citrus: The Florida Citrus Exchange*. Gainesville: University of Florida Press, 1959.

Lanier, Sidney. *Florida: Its Scenery, Climate and History*. Facsimile reproduction of the 1875 edition. Gainesville: University of Florida Press, 1973.

Laumer, Frank. *Massacre*. Gainesville: University of Florida Press, 1968.

Lazarus, William C. *Wings in the Sun: The Annals of Aviation in Florida*. Orlando: Cobb's, 1950.

Lowery, Woodbury. *The Spanish Settlements within the Present Limits of the United States*. Two volumes. New York: Putnam, 1901.

Lyon, Eugene. *The Enterprise of Florida*. Gainesville: University Presses of Florida, 1975.

Mahon, John D. *History of the Second Seminole War*. Gainesville: University of Florida Press, 1967.

Martin, Sidney W. *Florida During the Territorial Days*. Athens, Georgia: University of Georgia Press. 1944.

———. *Florida's Flagler*. Athens, Georgia: University of Georgia Press, 1949.

Milanich, Jerald T., and Charles H. Fairbanks. *Florida Archaeology*. New York: Academic Press, 1980.

Mormino, Gary R., and Anthony Pizzo. *Tampa: The Treasure City*. Tulsa: Continental Heritage Press, 1981.

Motte, Jacob Rhett. *Journey into Wilderness*. Edited by James E. Sunderman. Gainesville: University of Florida Press, 1963.

Mowat, Charles L. *East Florida as a British Province, 1763–1784*. Facsimile reproduction of the 1943 edition. Gainesville: University of Florida Press, 1964.

Parks, Arva Moore. *Miami: The Magic City*. Tulsa: Continental Heritage Press, 1981.

Patrick, Rembert W. *Florida Fiasco*. Athens, Georgia: University of Georgia Press, 1954.

Pettingill, George R. *Story of Florida Railroads, 1835–1903*. Boston: 1952.

Proctor, Samuel. *Napoleon Bonaparte Broward: Florida's Fighting Democrat*. Gainesville: University of Florida Press, 1950.

Redford, Polly. *Billion-Dollar Sandbar: A Biography of Miami Beach*. New York: E. P. Dutton and Co., 1970.

Shofner, Jerrell H. *Daniel Ladd: Merchant Prince of the Florida Frontier*. Gainesville: University Presses of Florida, 1978.

———. *Nor Is It Over Yet: Florida During the Era of Reconstruction, 1863–1877*. Gainesville: University of Florida Press, 1974.

——. *Orlando: The City Beautiful*. Tulsa: Continental Heritage Press, 1985.

Smith, Julia Floyd. *Slavery and Plantation Growth in Ante-Bellum Florida, 1821–1860*. Gainesville: University of Florida Press, 1973.

Solis de Meras, Gonzalo. *Pedro Menéndez de Avilés*. Facsimile reproduction of the 1567 manuscript. Translated by Jeanette Thurber Connor. Gainesville: University of Florida Press, 1964.

Sprague, John T. *The Florida War*. A facsimile reproduction of the 1848 edition. Gainesville: University of Florida Press, 1964.

Stockbridge, Frank Parker, and John Holliday Perry. *Florida in the Making*. Jacksonville: De Bower Publishing Co., 1926.

Swanton, John R. *Early History of the Creek Indians and Their Neighbors*. Bureau of American Ethnology. No. 73. Washington, D.C.: 1922.

——. *The Indians of the Southeastern United States*. Washington, D.C.: Government Printing Office, 1946.

Tebeau, Charlton W. *A History of Florida*. Coral Gables: University of Miami Press, 1971.

Vignoles, Charles. *Observations upon the Floridas*. Facsimile reproduction of the 1823 edition. Gainesville: University of Florida Press, 1977.

Ward, James R. *Old Hickory's Town: An Illustrated History of Jacksonville*. Jacksonville: Florida Publishing Co., 1982.

INDEX